M000283655

"Debbie is, first, a woman wi
are too quick to call themselv
them with a word that edifie
author keeps the focus on th
I recommend this read to all who want to serve the people of God."

Dr. Jim Hayford Sr., author, professor, preacher

"*The Gift of Prophetic Encouragement* demystifies the spiritual gift of prophesy by explaining what it is, what it is not and how God longs to breathe life, hope and healing into the lives of His children through the gift of prophetic encouragement. In a world that is so quick to focus on the negative, *The Gift of Prophetic Encouragement* is a breath of positive perspective straight from the heart of God for His children. Debbie repeatedly rests on the truth that God wants us to encourage one another, and she has done that from cover to cover. You will come away gently convicted, encouraged and ready to encourage!"

Dr. Michelle Bengtson, neuropsychologist; international speaker; author, *Hope Prevails: Insights from a Doctor's Personal Journey through Depression*

"Debbie Kitterman has written a balanced and instructive resource that will encourage followers of Jesus to live out their faith in a way that is desperately needed in today's culture. A truly prophetic lifestyle lived out in the character of Christ is the hope many are looking for. "

Rev. Tammy Dunahoo, vice president of U.S. operations/general supervisor, The Foursquare Church

"No doubt, we want to honor God and to love as Jesus loved. *The Gift of Prophetic Encouragement* helps us do just this. Debbie Kitterman trains us in the right way to encourage, inspire and share godly wisdom. The time is now to transform lives through the power of love."

Kelly Balarie, national speaker; blogger, Purposefulfaith.com; author, *Battle Ready: Train Your Mind to Conquer Challenges, Defeat Doubt and Live Victoriously* and *Fear Fighting*

"Be prepared to learn and be inspired! In her warm and engaging style, author Debbie Kitterman invites you to explore new ways to embrace a lifestyle of encouragement. Weaving biblical truth with compelling stories, this book will motivate you to joyfully respond to a rewarding and exciting adventure with God."

Judy Gordon Morrow, author, *The Listening Heart: Hearing God in Prayer*

"While Kitterman skillfully unpacks the concept of prophetic encouragement, it is a mistake to think that is all this book offers. Readers cannot help growing in their understanding of Scripture, falling more in love with Jesus and becoming excited to serve God through edifying and encouraging the Church. Absolutely brilliant!"

Robynne Elizabeth Miller, M.F.A.,
board president, Inspire Christian Writers

"Debbie's book on prophetic encouragement is super helpful! This resource will help you unlock both wisdom and encouragement on a daily basis!"

Sarah Bowling, founder, Saving Moses

"This book is for every believer who desires to hear from God to breathe His life, hope and healing into situations and people through the gift of prophetic encouragement. Debbie helps unpack the spiritual gifts so that we understand we are all prophetic! God is always speaking, and He desires for us to partner with Him to call forth things in others to remind them of His love and attention toward them. An authentic relationship with God blossoms when we can spread His joy and love by asking Him to use us to bless others with His message for them."

Tanya Jernigan, executive director, The Jernigan Foundation

"It's true! God wants to speak to you and through you every day. Debbie has lived and taught that in a way that is so inspiring and so practical for all of us. If you long for a faith that is both deep and part of daily life, you'll want to read and reread *The Gift of Prophetic Encouragement*."

Rich and Kirsten Root, pastors, Northwest Foursquare Church

"*The Gift of Prophetic Encouragement* is one of the most encouraging books I've read in a long time about the Holy Spirit's simple gift of prophecy. Like Debbie, too many people in traditional churches have hungered to hear the voice of God but have been told, 'It's not for today,' or, 'It's not for you.' Sharing her own journey, Debbie builds a beautiful bridge for people who desire to experience the supernatural voice of God, but in a grounded and biblical way. Her book is relatable and biblically sound, and it provides an excellent process for those who are hungry for more."

Jennifer Eivaz, founder, Harvest Ministries International;
author, *Seeing the Supernatural* and *The Intercessors Handbook*

The Gift of Prophetic Encouragement

Hearing the Words of God for Others

DEBBIE KITTERMAN

Chosen

a division of Baker Publishing Group
Minneapolis, Minnesota

© 2018 by Debbie Kitterman

Published by Chosen Books
11400 Hampshire Avenue South
Bloomington, Minnesota 55438
www.chosenbooks.com

Chosen Books is a division of
Baker Publishing Group, Grand Rapids, Michigan

Printed in the United States of America

ISBN 978-0-8007-9886-4

Library of Congress Control Number: 2018933920

Unless otherwise indicated, Scripture quotations are from the Holy Bible, New International Version®. NIV®. Copyright © 1973, 1978, 1984, 2011 by Biblica, Inc.™ Used by permission of Zondervan. All rights reserved worldwide. www.zondervan.com

Scripture quotations identified ESV are from The Holy Bible, English Standard Version® (ESV®), copyright © 2001 by Crossway, a publishing ministry of Good News Publishers. Used by permission. All rights reserved. ESV Text Edition: 2011

Scripture quotations identified MESSAGE are from THE MESSAGE. Copyright © by Eugene H. Peterson 1993, 1994, 1995, 1996, 2000, 2001, 2002. Used by permission of NavPress. All rights reserved. Represented by Tyndale House Publishers, Inc.

Scripture quotations identified NASB are from the New American Standard Bible®, copyright © 1960, 1962, 1963, 1968, 1971, 1972, 1973, 1975, 1977, 1995 by The Lockman Foundation. Used by permission. (www.Lockman.org)

Scripture quotations identified NKJV are from the New King James Version®. Copyright © 1982 by Thomas Nelson, Inc. Used by permission. All rights reserved.

Scripture quotations identified NLT are from the Holy Bible, New Living Translation, copyright © 1996, 2004, 2015 by Tyndale House Foundation. Used by permission of Tyndale House Publishers, Inc., Carol Stream, Illinois 60188. All rights reserved.

Scripture quotations identified KJV are from the King James Version of the Bible.

The personal testimonies included in this book are real; however, some names have been changed.

Cover design by Rob Williams, InsideOutCreativeArts

18 19 20 21 22 23 24   7 6 5 4 3 2 1

This book is dedicated to you!

Yes, *you*! As you read the pages of this book, I pray that my testimony and those of others will inspire you to be courageous. God is calling an army of ordinary people to rise up and release His love and heart to a world in desperate need. I pray this book would spark an awakening in the body of Christ, an opening of ears to hear the voice of God and a courage to step out in obedience to share His love with the world. It is time, Church. God is calling you. Awaken and arise!

God wants to communicate with us just as He did with Jesus when He walked on earth. Jesus' relationship with the Father is prophecy in action.

Contents

Foreword

The one who prophesies speaks to people for their strengthening, encouraging and comfort. . . . I would like every one of you to speak in tongues, but I would rather have you prophesy.

1 Corinthians 14:3, 5

Some things, like another pair of socks on Christmas morning, are added extras, but other gifts are much more than an optional luxury.

They are necessary gifts.

Like being rescued by a stranger when you are stranded in the middle of the night, or being caught after tripping headlong toward a cliff and saved from a fatal accident. These are *gifts* that can alter our future.

Archived in a safe place within the Library of Congress you will find an odd blue box. Written on the label are these words: *Contents of the President's pockets on the night of April 14, 1865.* History reminds us that this was the fateful night President Abraham Lincoln was assassinated. Among the items in the box, you will see a handkerchief embroidered *A. Lincoln*, a small pen knife, a pair of spectacles repaired with string and a

9

wallet containing a Confederate five-dollar bill and some worn newspaper articles. The newspaper clippings are most interesting. They report the great deeds of Abraham Lincoln. One of them records the declaration of John Bright, a British statesman, that Abraham Lincoln is one of the greatest men of all time.

Today, history tells us of the exploits, leadership, speeches and deeds of this great president, but in 1865, "history" hadn't been written yet. In 1865, Lincoln faced a divided nation. He struggled with soiled press reports of ineptitude, he debated with fierce critics and brutal opponents and he toiled tirelessly to restore a divided Union.

I can imagine the long nights in his study. There is something so moving about picturing a vulnerable president alone in a dimly lit Oval Office. Sitting at his desk, he'd reach into his pocket to read and reread the newspaper articles from an English statesman who declared that Lincoln was a great man. In the midst of his adversaries and doubts, those words refreshed and emboldened his heart. They gave him the courage and strength to go on, and today history heralds him as one of America's greatest presidents.

Everyone, even great leaders (as well as leaders *yet to be*), will face defining moments when they desperately need words of encouragement to go on.

God knew that.

He knew each of us would require a necessary gift that would enable us to fulfill His purpose in our lives. Moses reminds us of this. Scripture records his stunning legacy as one of Israel's greatest deliverers. Moses led two million Israelites out of slavery, wrote the Pentateuch and would appear with Jesus on the Mount of Transfiguration—yet there were times he was hanging by a thread, depleted and unsure. He needed a gift of prophetic encouragement. Then God raised up Jethro, Aaron and Hur.

David was known as the world's most gifted commander of covert operations, yet he would begin as an uncertain shepherd, unknown and anonymous. So God brought Samuel. We read about his great victories and exploits, yet hushed within the pages of 2 Samuel, we find him struggling outside Bethlehem, thirsty and exhausted. God raised up mighty men who encouraged and refreshed him.

Paul is the great apostle whose prolific pen God used to bring us much of the New Testament, yet there would be times when he was "troubled on every side; without were fightings, within were fears" (2 Corinthians 7:5 KJV). Then God brought Barnabas, and later, an obscure Onesiphorus, who refreshed Paul.

The gift of prophetic encouragement is a necessary gift, one that the Church is in great need of during these last days.

In *The Gift of Prophetic Encouragement*, Debbie Kitterman explains it well, but she does far more than that. She issues a call to those whom God is raising up, men and women through whom He will disburse the gift of prophetic encouragement. It is a necessary gift, and my prayer is that you will not only begin to recognize it, but become a part of it.

Please come in. The Kingdom of God has been waiting for you.

Dr. Wayne Cordeiro, president, New Hope Christian College; author, *The Divine Mentor*, *Leading on Empty* and more

Acknowledgments

There is an African proverb that says, "It takes a village to raise a child," that I think is also fitting for writing a book. In my opinion, a book is very much like raising a child; it is something that is the very best of who you are, poured out upon pages others will read. I could not have written this book without the prayers, love and support of my village. Thank you for gifting me with your encouragement, guidance and love.

For everyone who had a part in making this book a reality, thank you! Mere words cannot express the gratitude in my heart for you and your willingness to stand with me and cheer me on, so thank you from the bottom of my heart. This book holds my legacy and yours for this generation and the generations to come. I pray this book would cause an awakening in the body of Christ. May we all boldly step out in obedience to God and use the gift of prophetic encouragement to release the love of God.

Thank you to those who shared personal testimonies with me for use in the book. Most of your names have been changed, and others may never know who you are, but I do, and more importantly, God knows. I know many will be able to relate to what you shared, and I pray we can all glean and learn from each other's journey.

Thank you to those of you who read the early manuscript and gave feedback. Thank you for valuable input, thoughts and suggestions in making this the best book it could be. You have no idea how much it meant to me to have you be a part of this process. Also, special thanks to Kathy Marzolf for having an eagle eye and being a grammar guru. You are a wealth of knowledge when it comes to the English language.

To my husband, John: I thank God for you every single day. You have always been my biggest supporter and my champion. You are my knight in shining armor, always willing to go above and beyond to make sure I can say yes to the calling of God on my life and to the things I enjoy. Thank you for your hard work, sacrifice and dedication to God, to our family and to Restoration Church. I cannot imagine doing life or ministry without you by my side.

To my children, Jesse and Brandi: I love you, I am always for you and I believe in you. I will love you forever, and you will always be my babies, even when you have babies of your own. Never forget that. I know God has amazing things for you both as you continue to keep your eyes on Him. Thank you for your trust, your forgiveness for times when I was not the perfect mom, and for always giving me your support and love. You both have brought much joy to our family, and my life is so much richer with you both in it. God is about to do some amazing things and open doors for you both in this next season. Get ready!

Mom and Dad: Thank you, Mom, for being a persistent, powerful prayer warrior. I know your prayers are a large part of getting me to where I am today. Thank you for showing me that pursuing healing is a necessity if we are to live life to the fullest and for teaching me the power of saying, "I'm sorry." Dad, thank you for your love and support and for always being the proud dad of your kids and proud grandfather of your grandkids. I love you both so very much.

Thank you to the rest of my family and friends who have been so understanding and patient as I have been completely immersed in passionately pursuing my God calling and dream of writing. To my friends around the world and those living close by, you are all precious to me. Your faith and belief in me is what helped propel me forward, never to give up and to continue to share the message God has given me.

D2H Board: Thank you to all current and past Dare 2 Hear ministry board members, including Carl and Donna Sagerser, Ron and Patty Stoddard, Ben and Kate McDonald, Karter and Kathy Marzolf, and Pastor Jerry Tyler. You have stood beside me, believed in me and cheered me on when I needed it most. I am forever grateful for your friendship, your prayers, your wisdom and your support.

Pastor Jerry Tyler: Even though you are no longer here on the earth to share your love, support and wisdom, I want the world to know how much you meant to me. Dare 2 Hear ministry exists in large part due to your encouragement to step out. Thank you for believing in me and giving me a place to minister. You have left a huge legacy for those of us who called you pastor. Thank you for your obedience to Jesus and for entrusting John and me to carry your legacy forward with Restoration Church.

Restoration Church: Thank you for your love and support. Thank you for being our family and for sending me out all over the world with your blessing to minister to others in the body of Christ.

Melodi Stoddard and the D2H prayer shield team: Melodi, you are a godsend! Thank you for heading up my prayer partner ministry, but more importantly, thank you for being an amazing example of what it means to be a warrior woman of God. You do not back down, and you face challenges head on. I love your loyalty and the fierceness you have in protecting the ones you love. To the prayer shields: I am a firm believer that nothing advances in the kingdom without prayer, and truly much has been accomplished already. Thank you for being kingdom warriors and continuing to partner with me in prayer to see lives touched and miracles happen. I am excited to see what God does with the prayers of faith we have been praying for this book and the people who will read it.

Andy and Shannon Tate: Thank you both for your valuable input and help in working out a rearrangement solution and working with temperamental software. You are both a gift to John and me and Restoration Church. Andy, thank you for your graciousness and going with the flow when five minutes turned into five hours when Shannon and I would get carried away talking and working. Shannon, thank you for always going above and beyond the call of duty. Thank you for bringing your organization and administrative skills to our church and our lives. You help bring order to chaos, and I could not have fully dedicated the time I did and stepped away from some of my duties if you had not been here to fill in the gap. John and I are grateful for the gifts God has equipped you with, and we are humbled that He sent you to us. Thank you for reading, rereading and reading again each draft of the manuscript and giving valuable input and for being one of my biggest encouragers.

Kelly and Patti Krank: Thank you for always providing a place for me to write and serving as a home away from home from coast to coast. This book's journey began in the cottage on your property, the property that then became my family's home when you moved to the opposite coast. Patti, you have always been in my corner, and you are one of my biggest promoters. You have pushed me to be a better writer and blogger. You have always believed in me and inspired me. Thank you for pushing me to attend writers' conferences and even for making me sign up for an appointment with an editor. It looks like your encouragement was prophetic and spot on! It is your turn next, my friend. I can't wait for us both to be published authors.

Liz Curtis Higgs: Thank you for being a genuinely caring and loving person. Thank you for ministering to the one right in front of you and being obedient to God when He asked you to attend a conference to encourage your sisters in Christ even though you weren't a speaker or being paid to do so. Thank you for extending me the gift of your time and wisdom. You literally put courage into me the day we met, and your words propelled me forward with a new determination not to give up hope.

Kim Bangs: Thank you for believing in me and being sensitive to the prompting of the Holy Spirit. You are the real deal; you are genuine and personal. You are a truth teller but temper it with much love, and you made a scary process bearable. Thank you for being a visionary, taking a chance on an unknown writer and seeing the potential in this book and in me. I wouldn't want to be on this journey with anyone else!

Amanda Quain: I can't thank you enough for your attention to detail and your sensitivity to the Spirit. You made the editing process a lot less painful than I had imagined it would be, and you definitely brought out the best in my writing! Thank you for partnering with the Holy Spirit and lending me your talents to make this book the best it can be. I have been incredibly blessed by you. Though we have never met face-to-face, I know you are one amazing woman! I pray our paths cross again one day.

The team at Chosen Books and Baker Publishing: Thank you for taking a chance on me and believing in the message God has given me to share. Thank you for walking me through every step of the process with much grace and understanding.

To my heavenly Father, Jesus and the Holy Spirit: I am forever grateful for Your love, grace and mercy! Thank You for fully equipping me to do the work You have set before me. I am humbled by how You helped me dream again and embrace the call to be a writer. Even when doubt, fear and discouragement from others came, You continued to place people in my life to speak prophetic encouragement and truth to me. You are my Champion, my Healer and my Friend. You are amazing at opening doors. Thank You for never giving up on me and staying true to the promises of Your Word. Holy Spirit, thank You for breathing inspiration into my writing and allowing me to partner with You to write this book. You are always good and always faithful.

Introduction

God longs for His people to use the gifts He has given them, especially the gift of prophecy. The spiritual gift of prophecy (see appendix 1) is speaking Holy Spirit–inspired words of edification, exhortation or comfort to individuals. Prophetic encouragement is something every follower of Christ can give to others in his or her day-to-day life. This simple truth opens our eyes to the ordinary nature of prophecy, which breathes life, love and hope into the dry places of our lives.

While recently attending a conference, I was sitting by ladies I had met a few days prior. One turned to me and said, "I know what you do. I've been stalking you on Facebook." I was thinking she was probably shocked to discover I am a pastor. I laughed and asked her what it was I did that was so fascinating. "You operate in the prophetic, and we want a prophetic word."

It did not even cross my mind to think she was talking about the fact that I operate in the prophetic. I do not hide it, but it is not something I broadcast on Facebook. It is part of who I am. My response was said in laughter: "The prophetic isn't like a slot machine where you make a demand and out pops a message. However, God is always speaking, and I am sure He has some encouragement for you."

They laughed and thought the conversation ended because the session began. But it was not the end of the conversation. During the session the Lord began showing me His heart for these women. As soon as I could, I shared with the ladies what God had shown me. They both walked away blessed and knew without a doubt God was real. He loved them, He knew them by name, and He cared about their concerns.

Prophetic messages are more than validation, reassurances or knowledge of what the future holds. God longs to breathe life, hope and healing into the lives of His children through the gift of prophetic encouragement. He wants us all to be available to speak His words to those we meet, regardless of their relationship with God.

As I sat in an airport restaurant working on this book, I was reminded how much God loves those who do not yet have a relationship with Him. I was waiting for my server, Seth, to return when I glanced up and saw him. Instantly, a picture of a little girl flashed in my mind. The Lord whispered to my heart, *He's got a heavy heart concerning his daughter.* I thought to myself, *I don't even know if he has a daughter.* I continued to work but was mindful of Seth's whereabouts. He was laughing and joking and seemed to be having an awesome day, not a heavy heart. I thought to myself, *I am going to have to step out in faith and trust that God wants me to encourage this young man. If he doesn't have a daughter, I know God will give me an encouraging word.*

Finally, he returned to my table, and I politely asked if he had a little girl. He looked at me funny and said he did indeed have a daughter. He stared at me with a puzzled look, a look that said, "How did you know?" Before he could ask, I told him he had caught my attention from across the restaurant, and I felt God showed me he had a heavy heart for his little girl. I went on to share the heaviness had to do with a financial need, and he nodded his head in agreement. I shared more of what God revealed to me. He was extremely grateful and kept thanking me. I had not done anything extraordinary; I simply had responded to what God was showing me. This is exactly what Jesus modeled in every encounter we read about in the New Testament.

When I read the stories of Jesus' great adventures I am struck by how clearly He showed us exactly what it looks like to embrace a lifestyle of encouragement. Jesus had radical encounters with ordinary people every day. By listening to the Father's voice and doing what the Father said, Jesus was able to release heaven into the situations and lives of those He encountered.

You may recall the biblical stories when God provided the Israelites with manna and quail to sustain them in the desert (see Exodus 16:13–15, 35; Psalm 105:40; John 6:31). He did the same for John the Baptist by providing honey and locusts (see Matthew 3:4). And Jesus? His sustenance came through the very words and pictures God gave Him. This is the same encouragement Jesus then shared with others. His words of encouragement were filled with truth, life and hope. These prophetic messages were spoken to the brokenhearted and the lost for the purpose of drawing them closer to God.

When Jesus interacted with people, He fulfilled and renewed the meaning of what was written in Old Testament Scriptures: "Jesus answered by quoting Deuteronomy [8:3]: 'It takes more than bread to stay alive. It takes a steady stream of words from God's mouth'" (Matthew 4:4 MESSAGE).

There is a difference between our human words of encouragement and those empowered by the Spirit. We can empathize and encourage others when they seem down, upset or sad. We can even pray for them to be encouraged and ask God to comfort them. Yet we do not always know or see that someone needs encouragement. Such was the case with Seth. From all appearances, Seth acted like everything was right in his world. Had God not interrupted my thoughts and showed me what I could not see in the natural, I would have missed an opportunity to encourage someone with the love of God.

The gift of prophetic encouragement requires us to hear and see things from God's perspective. Once we do that, we can speak His language, which is love and encouragement to others. This is the prophetic gift of encouragement in action. The messages God gives are hope-filled and life-giving, and even more so when they are exactly what the person needs in that moment. They are not our best intentions; they are God's words and His intentions for the individual. God knows what someone is going through, He knows exactly what they need, and He's looking for someone to be a willing and available vessel to speak through. Are you ready to be that someone? Keep reading.

The truth is we are all prophetic, which simply means we can all hear from God. In the New Testament, Paul tells us the spiritual gift of prophecy is for all:

> Follow the way of love and eagerly desire gifts of the Spirit, especially prophecy. . . . But the one who prophesies speaks to people for their strengthening, encouraging and comfort. . . . I would rather have you prophesy.
>
> 1 Corinthians 14:1, 3, 5

God speaks to us today like He did from the beginning. God desires a two-way conversation. I believe—no, I know—God wants to speak directly to His children, and He wants His children to speak directly to Him. God has given us *all* the gift of prophecy, and as we walk with Him daily He wants us to embrace a lifestyle of speaking encouragement to others we meet: "Therefore encourage one another and build one another up, just as you are doing" (1 Thessalonians 5:11 ESV).

God's messages or "words" (see appendix 1) come to us directly through reading the Bible and through prophetic words in the form of comfort, strength and encouragement. In prophetic circles, "a word" can mean any message from God represented as an impression, picture, vision, Scripture or a literal word.

For some, the prophetic is yet to be experienced. For others, the prophetic is rare and random. There are even some who have been hurt by the misuse and abuse of prophecy. Yet, the prophetic needs to be a part of our everyday lives. We need to listen to the Lord, we need to respond when He asks us to do something, and we need to speak encouragement to others as He directs.

I do not know about you, but I do not think I am super special. In fact, I view my life as normal. You could say I am ordinary, like you. Yet, I am also radical. When I partner with the Holy Spirit and allow Him to move in my ordinary life, radical things happen. I become bold. I become brave. I step out of my fears and lean into the Father's heart for others. I embrace operating in a lifestyle of encouragement. I have simply learned how to tune in to the frequency of heaven for the purpose of receiving these prophetic messages, or words, with the intent of encouraging others. Everyone can use encouragement, comfort and strengthening daily.

God's Word tells why encouragement is necessary in Hebrews 3:13 (NASB): "But encourage one another day after day, as long as it is still called 'Today,' *so that none of you will be hardened by the deceitfulness of sin*" (emphasis added).

We are called to be beacons of light and hope in a dying world. This world is lost, and Jesus is the answer! We need to remember that when we speak, our words greatly affect us and those around us. Good words spoken to us meet our basic need to love and be loved. Therefore, when we embrace the lifestyle of encouragement, we are operating in God's original design of life-giving prophecy.

This is the gift of prophetic encouragement.

Activation Prayer

Dear Lord Jesus, thank You for Your Holy Spirit, who leads me into all truth. Jesus, I give You permission to search my heart and mind. Show me places where I have preconceived ideas or prejudices, especially when it comes to understanding prophecy. Create a hunger in me to be radical for the Kingdom of God. Open my ears, eyes, heart and mind to receive fresh revelation from You today.

Note to the Reader

This book is designed to give you an interactive experience. Throughout the book you will find personal reflection questions in Go Deeper sections, as well as Activation Prayers and Activate Encouragement exercises.* The Think on It! sections guide you deeper than the personal reflection questions. Last, you will find testimonies designed to build your faith and increase boldness in the Encouragement in Action sections.

---

*Activate Encouragement exercises are simple activities designed to help you become familiar with the process of hearing God's voice. They are structured to provide a safe environment for you to experience a variety of methods that God uses to speak to people.

1

Open Invitation

I have spent a great deal of my life trying to figure out how to connect genuinely with God. I kept waiting by my mailbox for Him to send me an invitation. The truth is, my invitation had already arrived. I simply had to RSVP.

Authentic relationship with God is about spending time with Him, hearing from Him, listening to Him, responding to Him. Throughout Scripture there are examples of what authentic relationships look like between God and His people. It is not only about going to church, worshiping, reading the Word or praying. It is about experiencing a two-way conversation.

In the beginning, literally, God set the model of relationship with Adam and Eve. This intimacy with God gave them an open dialogue with the Father at all times. Jesus' relationship with the Father is exactly the same. Jesus has full access, and it is the same for you and me.

Jesus shared how God speaks directly to His Spirit. He said, "I only do and say what My Father does and says" (see John 5:19; 8:28; 12:49–50). This is not an exclusive conversation reserved for the Creator and His Son. This is our relationship goal with God. When Jesus walked on the earth, He was both fully God and fully human. This distinction is vital to understanding that we are co-heirs with Christ (see Romans 8:17).

Jesus laid down His divine nature and walked on earth. He walked in our shoes to show us we have access to the Kingdom of heaven. We can lay hands on the sick and see them healed. We can hear God's voice and prophesy. We can pray and see miracles in action. We have a relationship with the Father by communicating directly with Him. Jesus demonstrated this communication when He implored God to take the burden of the cross from Him (see Luke 22:42). Even though we do not hear the other side of the conversation in the Scriptures, we know God answered Jesus by dispatching an angel to comfort Him (see Luke 22:43).

God wants a true and intimate connection directly with His people. Adam and Eve had this connection with God in the Garden. From the very beginning of creation God desired relationship, so He created mankind. God gave them dominion over the earth, as well as knowledge and access to the thoughts and heart of the Father. They had a deep connection with one another until Satan slithered in and mucked it up.

True relationships are powerful and destructive to the enemy, so Satan set out to destroy Adam and Eve's fellowship with God. Satan first approached Eve with questions crafted to twist the truth of God's mandate regarding the forbidden fruit. In doing so, Satan launched a full-out assault on man's relationship with God. Adam and Eve disobeyed, and the result was a broken relationship with God and spiritual death.

Originally, Satan (also called Lucifer, the Daystar or the Son of the Morning) was an archangel created by God to be the angel of worship. He was the covering angel created to dwell eternally in the throne room in the presence of God: "You were anointed as a guardian cherub, for so I ordained you. You were on the holy mount of God; you walked among the fiery stones" (Ezekiel 28:14).

Lucifer's problem was he wanted to be an equal with God, and God does not share glory. He was stripped of his beauty, wisdom and position and cast from heaven.

> How you have fallen from heaven, morning star, son of the dawn! You have been cast down to the earth, you who once laid low the nations! You said in your heart, "I will ascend to the heavens; I will raise my throne above the stars of God; I will sit enthroned on the mount of assembly, on the utmost heights of Mount Zaphon. I will ascend above the tops of the clouds; I will make myself like the Most High." But you are brought down to the realm of the dead, to the depths of the pit.
>
> Isaiah 14:12–15

Because of his jealousy, Satan set out to destroy mankind's personal relationship with God. If he could not have a relationship with God, then he would make sure no one did.

Satan's idea of relationship is a dictatorship leading to slavery and bondage. His attack is direct: divide a household so it cannot stand. This is why we see such an assault against healthy relationships in our world today.

> Jesus knew their thoughts and said to them, "Every kingdom divided against itself will be ruined, and every city or household divided against itself will not stand."
>
> Matthew 12:25

God's Relational Character

God reveals His relational character to Adam and Eve in Genesis 2:4 by using a different name. Wait, what? He uses a different name? Genesis 2:4 tells us, "This is the account of the heavens and the earth when they were created, when the Lord God made the earth and the heavens."

The references to God in the verses leading up to this passage refer to the deity of God as the transcendent* Creator. This is an image of God that is distant and conceptual. In Genesis 2:4, however, we see God's personal name being used, "the Lord God." In the original Hebrew language, it is represented as *Yahweh*. This is a significant shift from the formal use of "God the Creator" to His relational name, Yahweh. The use of God's personal name is important and illuminates the relational nature of God.

Again, in Genesis 3:1 when the serpent addresses Eve, he does not use God's personal name, Yahweh, but addresses Him as God:

> Now the serpent was more crafty than any of the wild animals the Lord God had made. He said to the woman, "Did God really say, 'You must not eat from any tree in the garden'?"

What is your view of God? Do you see Him as personal and relational, or is He distant and indifferent? It matters how you view Him. It affects everything about your relationship with Him.

I first met Jodi at a workshop I taught. She was having a hard time understanding some concepts I was sharing, but she wanted to know the truth of who God was. Jodi shared that she came from a background that viewed God as a distant authoritarian figure. She did not know or believe God knew her personally

---

*According to Dictionary.com, *transcendent* means "going beyond ordinary limits; surpassing; exceeding; superior or supreme; Theology. (of the Deity) transcending the universe, time, etc. Compare *immanent*."

Transcendent is "a theological term referring to the relation of God to creation. God is 'other,' 'different' from His creation. He is independent and different from His creatures (Isaiah 55:8–9). He transcends His creation. He is beyond it and not limited by it or to it" ("Meaning of Transcendence," *Bible.org*, https://bible.org/illustration/meaning-transcendence).

or that He spoke today. But she always felt there was more and was on a spiritual journey desiring to learn more about God.

Later, while Jodi took my classes, she came to understand God does speak today through the ordinary and even mundane. She realized He saw her as an individual and wanted an even deeper relationship with her than she thought possible. As Jodi was awakened to a deeper relationship with God, she felt more cherished, loved and chosen by Him. She felt her view of God shift, and she came to know Him as a real, personal Savior.

She now understands that God was not looking to punish; instead, He was lifting her up and showing her He loved her in a million different ways. Jodi said to me, referring to the Parable of the Lost Sheep (see Luke 15:1–7), "It has made all the difference in my relationship and how I interact with God. I do not come from a place of judgment or anger, or even from a place where I am not good enough. Instead, I now know I am the one He left the ninety-nine for! God is pursuing me, and He's pursuing others as well. You and I, we are the one."

God Wants Restoration

Jesus' life on earth, His death and His resurrection restored our relationship with God: "He will turn the hearts of the parents to their children, and the hearts of the children to their parents" (Malachi 4:6). But in order to have an authentic relationship characterized by intimacy and communication, like Adam and Eve experienced with God in the Garden, we need the Spirit of God. On the Day of Pentecost God poured out His Holy Spirit (see Acts 2:2–14, 17–18) on the people and in an instant restored the final piece necessary to reestablish communication with the Father.

Through salvation and grace, we too have access to the Father when we choose to be in relationship with Him. Once we have our eyes focused on God and our relationship with Him is firmly established, God will use us in each other's lives. God wants people who are willing to hear, who can be trusted and who are in relationship with others. We need God, and we need each other.

Go Deeper

- Do you have a difficult time connecting with God? If yes, why do you think that is?

- How do John 5:19; 8:28; 12:49–50 apply to you today?

- If Jesus is our model for relationship with the Father, what can you learn and implement from His example?

- Why is the Holy Spirit the vital piece to restore our relationship with the Father?

- What image comes to mind when you think of God?

- Do you have a personal relationship with Jesus Christ? One where you have personally asked Him to be Lord of your life?

If your answer to the last question above is yes, congratulations! If not, this book is about incorporating the gift of prophetic encouragement into your everyday life. For that to happen you need to have a relationship with God, the Creator of the universe, but you also need to come to know Him as Yahweh.

If you have not said yes to a personal relationship with Jesus, or if you have walked away from Him, I implore you to enter into a real relationship with Him. You will find a prayer to do this in appendix 2.

Activation Prayer

Father God, I say yes to Your invitation to go deeper with You today. Help me to see You as more than just the Creator of the universe. I'm tired of not living in the fullness of relationship You have to offer. God, show me how to authentically connect with You. I ask for full restoration of relationship with You. God, touch and heal any misbeliefs in me that have created a wrong perception of who You really are. Help my eyes to stay focused on You and establish a strong, firm foundation built upon the truths found in Your Word.

Activate Encouragement

Real, authentic relationship involves a two-way conversation. When you need some advice or want to spend time with a friend, what do you do? You usually share a meal, talk on the phone or meet for coffee. I know this may seem strange, but I want you to invite Jesus to sit with you and visit over a cup of coffee or tea.

In your home, pull up an extra chair at the table or make room on your couch and invite Jesus to join you. Begin by sharing with Him about the things on your mind concerning your day. Then listen for Him to respond. More than likely you will not hear the audible voice of God—that is rare—but God can answer through your thoughts and give you His ideas or whisper Scriptures of encouragement to you. He may even bring to mind a sermon, a podcast, an article or another message you read or heard someone speak.

2

Direct Access

Relationships are a vital part of who we are and how we exist, yet they are one of the most difficult aspects of our lives. In an effort to find our way, we often enlist others to help us approach God. Unfortunately, when we do this, we are falling into the same pattern that kept the children of Israel from a restored relationship with the Father.

Examine Moses' role. God was seeking a direct relationship with His people, but the Israelites were afraid and begged for the security of a middleman. God, in His goodness, desired more for the Israelites. He revealed His plans to deliver the Israelites out of the desert and to reestablish a direct, personal relationship with them.

> "'Now if you obey me fully and keep my covenant, then out of all nations you will be my treasured possession. Although the whole earth is mine, you will be for me a kingdom of priests and a holy nation.' These are the words you are to speak to the Israelites." . . . And the LORD said to Moses, "Go to the people and consecrate them today and tomorrow."
>
> Exodus 19:5–6, 10

In the verses above, we clearly read that God wanted the Israelites to become a kingdom of priests. Every person, from priest to commoner, would be consecrated (see Exodus 19:21–22) and set apart for God.

God had one restriction: The people were not to approach the mountain until the proper time. When the ram's horn blew, each Israelite would be consecrated as a priest and fully authorized to approach God (see Exodus 19:12–13). On the third day, Moses led the people to the base of the mountain. As God called Moses to return up the mountain, the people witnessed lightning and smoke and heard the blast of trumpets. Overcome with fear, they called to Moses from a distance, saying, "Speak to us yourself and we will listen. But do not have God speak to us or we will die" (Exodus 20:19).

Moses replied:

> "Do not be afraid. God has come to test you, so that the fear of God will be with you to keep you from sinning." The people remained at a distance, while Moses approached the thick darkness where God was.
>
> Exodus 20:20–21

God's specific purpose for Moses was to deliver His people to the Promised Land, not be the mediator. God wanted to reestablish a direct relationship with them; yet in their fear they inadvertently chose to continue their broken relationship with God. This is the bitter inheritance that was handed down to future generations until the arrival of Jesus Christ.

After generations of priests serving as mediators and then four hundred years of silence, God sent Jesus to reconcile mankind back to God once and for all. Jesus modeled an unhindered relationship with the Father. He taught us how to relate to Him first and to one another second. He demonstrated hearing the Father speak. He told His disciples we could do the same things

He did (see John 14:12). When we partner with the Father we too can heal the sick, cleanse the leper and set the captives free.

As Jesus neared the end of His earthly ministry, He gave His disciples a new command to "abide in Me" (John 15:4 NKJV). This is an invitation to a much deeper relationship with Him. The Parable of the Vine and the Branches in John 15 is a great biblical example of what it means to have a deeper, more intimate relationship with God.

> I am the true vine, and My Father is the vinedresser. Every branch in Me that does not bear fruit He takes away; and every branch that bears fruit He prunes, that it may bear more fruit. You are already clean because of the word which I have spoken to you. Abide in Me, and I in you. As the branch cannot bear fruit of itself, unless it abides in the vine, neither can you, unless you abide in Me. I am the vine, you are the branches. He who abides in Me, and I in him, bears much fruit; for without Me you can do nothing. If anyone does not abide in Me, he is cast out as a branch and is withered; and they gather them and throw them into the fire, and they are burned. If you abide in Me, and My words abide in you, you will ask what you desire, and it shall be done for you. By this My Father is glorified, that you bear much fruit; so you will be My disciples.
>
> John 15:1–8 NKJV

This passage is full of powerful promises for us if we abide in Him. Even though the pruning process does not sound pleasant, it is necessary to sustain life, new growth and an abundant crop. His Word promises that if we remain (abide) in Him we will bear much fruit, and when we ask for the things we desire they will be given. It is not selfish, fleshly desires we will be asking for but the desires that the Spirit of God releases to us as we abide in and stay connected to Jesus.

After Jesus' resurrection He spent time with the disciples to prepare them for what lay ahead. It was vital for what was

35

to come that they have a solid relationship with Him and each other. Jesus would soon give them their Great Commission: to help build His Church once He returned to heaven. Just like those early disciples, we can hear His voice, and we are called to carry out that same commission to go into all the earth to be His witnesses (see Matthew 28:19; Mark 16:15), furthering His Kingdom until He returns.

Jesus teaches us we have direct access to the Father. No middleman is required. Nonetheless, many believers struggle to walk out this truth in their daily lives. Have you ever felt you needed someone else to be a mediator or a middleman in your relationship with God? If so, you are not alone. My friend Shannon did not fully understand she could hear God speak, let alone that He would want to speak to her. Shannon shared her story with me:

> Years ago, I volunteered as an usher at a leadership conference packed full of famous pastors and notable authors of faith. One night they opened up a prayer and healing session for the attendees. My role that night was to direct folks to the next available prayer person. Lines formed almost immediately; thus began a three-hour prayer session!
>
> Once all the attendees went through, it was the volunteers' turn to receive prayer. I excitedly thought, *If anyone can talk to God, it will be these guys! I need to hear God's plans for me.* One by one, I was getting passed over. Ministers started leaving, and the famous pastors had gone for the night. I finally approached the last pastor standing, who said, "Well, are you coming back tomorrow? We can pray for you then."
>
> I was literally the only one left in the sanctuary, and I felt I was given an IOU. I didn't even make it home before I sat down on the curb and sobbed. I thought God didn't want me to hear what He had to say. It took years of healing and talking with folks with similar stories to realize God didn't want to use someone else to talk to me; He wanted to talk to me directly! I realized the error of my thinking. God wanted me to talk to

Him as I would talk to any of my friends or family, and He wanted to talk to me.

Now I go for prayer to get confirmation of what I heard God say, not to hear God.

The one and only thing that gets in the way of our relationship with the Father is us! If we repent of our sins and confess with our mouth that Jesus Christ is Lord (see Romans 10:9; 1 John 1:9), then we are born again—saved, a believer in Jesus Christ, one of His disciples. But most of us stop at this point. We camp at comfortable instead of seeking a deeper, more intimate relationship with the Father. We follow our friends on Facebook, believing it is real friendship. It is not. Similarly, if we merely follow Jesus, then we are truly missing out on real relationship. When Jesus sacrificed Himself for us, the pathway to genuine relationship was restored. Christ's death and resurrection means we can all enter into the presence of God face-to-face.

Go Deeper

- Are you afraid to have God speak to you? Why or why not?

- Do you feel you have direct access to Father God? Or do you believe you need someone else to approach Him for you? Explain.

- Read John 15:1–17 (NKJV). What do you think it means to abide in Christ?

- What would it look like in your life for you to abide in Him?

Activation Prayer

Dear Jesus, help me not to be comfortable with the status quo. Instead, create in me a desire to seek a deeper, more intimate relationship with the Father. I do not want to be just a follower; I want to be Your disciple and Your friend. I want to abide in You. Jesus, help me see my shortcomings. Your Word promises that You will be a light to my path (see Psalm 119:35). Place my feet on the pathway (see Psalm 25:4) to genuine relationship with You. Jesus, I invite You to come meet with me face-to-face (see Deuteronomy 5:4), just as You did with Adam, Eve and Moses and just as You intended since the beginning. Amen!

Activate Encouragement

Set aside a specific time to spend with the Lord today. Don't come with any set expectations, needs or demands. Come to Him as you are! As you begin your time with Him, make sure to pray the above prayer again out loud. Then begin your time together by playing worship music and singing along. In your own way, express to the Lord how much He means to you and your love for Him. Then journal about your experience, making sure to note anything specific He may have spoken to your heart.

Think on It!

The Torn Curtain

Scripture tells us the curtain of the temple was torn at Jesus' death: "At that moment the curtain of the temple was torn in two from top to bottom. The earth shook, the rocks split" (Matthew 27:51).

Within the temple there were two rooms: the outer room, called the holy place, and the inner, most sacred room, called the most holy place or the holy of holies. The holy of holies was the one place where God's presence dwelled on earth. Separating the most holy place from the outer room was a curtain that hung sixty feet high and spread thirty feet wide. The curtain was an elaborate woven fabric made of four colors: blue, purple, scarlet and white (linen). (See Exodus 26:31.) Common people were prohibited from entering the holy of holies. Only the high priest entered once a year on the Day of Atonement (see Leviticus 16:2–34). The curtain separating these two places was a looming, physical reminder of the separation between God and His people.

It is significant that the curtain specifically tore from top to bottom, from heaven to earth, when Christ was crucified. This represented the end of the separation between God and His people. Because of Christ's obedience to the cross, His presence was released into the world through the Holy Spirit. No longer are we separated from God! We have direct access to enter into the very throne room of God—the holy of holies—where God and His glory dwell (see Hebrews 6:19–20; 10:19–22). Although the true holy of holies is in heaven, God's presence is no longer confined to a location (see Acts 1:8; 10:36–38; 1 Corinthians 2:10–16).

Activation Prayer

Thank You, Jesus, for Your sacrifice and giving Your life so I would no longer be separated from God. I am grateful for Your sacrifice. Father God, I ask You to open my eyes to see You and to know the truth that I now have total access to You through Your Son, Jesus. Lord, let Your glory fall in my life and give me the confidence to enter boldly into the throne room of God so we can meet face-to-face.

--- **Go Deeper** ---

- Read Hebrews 10:19–22.

- How does this Scripture say we are to enter into the holy of holies (the most holy place)?

- What does this Scripture say about the significance of the curtain? What does this mean for you personally?

3

God Speaks Today

Growing up, I lacked the language to define what I was sensing in my spirit. I experienced a great deal of confusion between the world I could see and touch and the world I could sense. The leaders of my church offered a diet of conservative, foundational, biblical Christian teaching but limited discussions concerning the spiritual gifts, especially prophecy. This unbalanced diet defined my spiritual boundaries.

I believe there are many whose spiritual boundaries are defined by the same things that defined mine. I know there are people who have the same hunger I did.

My friend Patti was brought up in a conservative evangelical church that was strong in the Word, but she felt something was missing. She hungered for more. In her search for answers she began to listen to sermons on the radio, research the Scriptures and attend a weekly Bible study. In her quest for truth Patti came to the conclusion that what she read in the Bible and what some Bible teachers were saying did not always align. In her pursuit for more she heard a message from Jack Hayford. Her initial response was, "He believes like I do." To her, Pastor

41

Jack confirmed what she knew all along: Spiritual gifts did not cease when Jesus ascended into heaven. In her words, "I already believed in my spirit that the gifts were for today, and then I heard someone who validated what I was already sensing in my spirit." God still speaks today, and His gifts are very much alive and working in the body of believers.

I often tell people I am the most normal prophetic person they may ever meet. I may have been born *knowing*, but I did not know what I knew. I felt as though my conservative church gave me a recipe for life, but a key ingredient was missing. Maybe this is your story too; maybe you are on the quest for more of God and a deeper relationship with Him, as I was.

My first steps to a deeper relationship started when I was 25 years old. I prayed a prayer that changed my life forever. I asked God for three things: a new church, a new house and a new job for my husband. Before I say more, let me give you some background.

I grew up in a church where the raising of hands in worship or shouting, "Amen!" was not only discouraged, it was off-limits. We believed in the fruit of the Spirit but not certain gifts of the Spirit.

I can recall several occasions when I asked my youth pastor about the gifts of speaking in tongues and prophecy. The response was always the same: "We don't really teach on those here." One specific time my youth leader took me aside out of sheer exasperation and told me, "Our denomination doesn't believe in those particular gifts. Those things happened a long time ago and aren't happening today. We will not be taking time to talk about them again!" Needless to say, I never brought up the subject again, but I always felt as if I was missing out. I hungered for something more. I had no idea what the "more" was, but I was committed to find it. At 25 I earnestly began to pray for a new church.

My second prayer was for a new house. Our 980-square-foot home was too small for our family of four. Our son and daughter were growing quickly. Sharing rooms is not a problem when kids are little, but I knew they would need their own rooms eventually. With our limited budget, however, it would take a miracle.

My third prayer was for my husband, John, to get a new job. I was a stay-at-home mom, and we were a one-income family. When John's boss left, they asked him to take on her responsibilities in addition to his own. His hours increased and his stress level increased, but his pay stayed the same. It was hard on our family and our marriage.

I prayed earnestly while creating my own perfect plan. First, God would provide a better job for my husband, which would logically lead to a new home and eventually lead us to a new church. I had it all worked out! All God would have to do is cooperate. Done and done! But God, in His sovereignty, saw fit to make His own plan for my life.

John was offered a new job in another state, and we relocated. What was God thinking? In spite of what appeared to be a complete answer to my heartfelt prayers, I was seriously angry with God. People say, "Be careful what you pray for," for a reason. I had never lived more than an hour away from my family; now I was four hours away. No more free babysitting. Worse yet, I didn't know a single person. This was not what I had prayed for! I truly felt alone, yet God knew exactly what I needed. It took two years from the time I prayed my life-changing prayers to realize it, but eventually I came to understand that God had answered my requests, just not according to my plans.

Several months after we moved—though long before my realization about God's hand on our situation—we settled in and found a new church. I began attending a Bible study and was invited to the annual women's retreat. I was happy to go, but I was out of my comfort zone. This new church was nothing like our old church. I was not sure what to expect at the retreat. It was a Spirit-filled denomination that operated in the gifts of the Spirit.

During a morning session at the retreat the pastor's wife announced she wanted us to spend time seeking God and writing down what we heard Him say. I thought she was crazy. I had never heard of such a thing. God was going to speak to me? I had no idea if this could really happen. I decided if God was really going to speak to me, then I wanted to have an honest conversation. During the process I let God have it. I told Him exactly what I was feeling: *Why did You move me away from everything I have ever known? Why have You abandoned me? Why are You not saying anything?* The list went on and on. I didn't hear a response from God, but I realized I did feel better.

The next day on the ride back home, I was exhausted. Since there were only three of us in the van, I was free to lie down in the back seat for a nap. I am not really sure how much time had passed, but suddenly I was wide-awake. "Didn't I give you everything you prayed for?" asked an audible voice. I could not make sense of what I heard.

I assumed it was either something from the radio seeping into my dream or the two ladies in the front talking. I asked them, "Did either of you say, 'Didn't I give you everything you asked for?'" In stereo, they both said, "No." The lady driving looked at me in the rearview mirror. She laughed and said, "We've been talking, and you were sleeping the entire time."

I was genuinely confused. It is hard to believe I could miss something so clear, but at the time I was completely lost. It would be almost two years later before I understood God had spoken to me. Not only did He speak to me loud and clear, but He also answered my heated questions. Until that moment, I did not understand God still speaks today. But suddenly I found the missing ingredient: For the first time I had spoken to God the way I would speak to a friend. He replied more than 24 hours later, but I will never forget it, nor could I miss it.

The Old Testament tells us a similar story in 1 Samuel 3:1–10 (ESV):

Now the boy Samuel was ministering to the LORD in the presence of Eli. And the word of the LORD was rare in those days; there was no frequent vision. At that time Eli, whose eyesight had begun to grow dim so that he could not see, was lying down in his own place. The lamp of God had not yet gone out, and Samuel was lying down in the temple of the LORD, where the ark of God was. Then the LORD called Samuel, and he said, "Here I am!" and ran to Eli and said, "Here I am, for you called me." But he said, "I did not call; lie down again." So he went and lay down. And the Lord called again, "Samuel!" and Samuel arose and went to Eli and said, "Here I am, for you called me." But he said, "I did not call, my son; lie down again." Now Samuel did not yet know the LORD, and the word of the LORD had not yet been revealed to him. And the LORD called Samuel again the third time. And he arose and went to Eli and said, "Here I am, for you called me." Then Eli perceived that the LORD was calling the boy. Therefore Eli said to Samuel, "Go, lie down, and if he calls you, you shall say, 'Speak, LORD, for your servant hears.'" So Samuel went and lay down in his place. And the LORD came and stood, calling as at other times, "Samuel! Samuel!" And Samuel said, "Speak, for your servant hears."

I have always wondered why God chose to speak to Samuel. After all, he was only a child. But God does not look at age or position. We must understand God's choice to speak with Samuel was based on faith and obedience, not a chain of command.

Scripture says, "The word of the Lord was rare in those days." Therefore, when God called Samuel's name, he immediately thought it was Eli, the priest. Why didn't he know it was God? Because there is a difference between having knowledge of God and knowing God. Samuel had knowledge of who God was, but he did not yet have a personal relationship with the Lord.

Just like Samuel, I did not initially recognize God's voice. On some level I recognized that God had spoken to me, but I was still so full of doubt and confusion. My revelation was short-lived, and the doubt eventually won out. I remained in the dark about who I was in God's eyes.

I have come to realize God sees the bigger picture. He knew I needed to relocate to a new place first before He could answer my next two prayers. He knows my destiny and my dreams, as He does yours. We often fail, however, to step into what God is calling us to do because we do not recognize His voice. Later I will discuss the various ways we can hear Him speaking to us, but please know most people do not often hear the audible voice of God like Samuel or even I did. Instead, it is more often God-inspired thoughts, impressions or pictures in our mind. These expressions of the prophetic are no less valid or spiritual than that audible voice; they are no less "real" and should be no less impactful in our lives.

So how do we fine-tune our hearing so we do not miss it when God speaks to us, whatever form it may take? To best hear from God we need to be in relationship with Him and be willing to take action when He speaks. The key is first knowing, then listening, and finally responding in obedience to His voice. Do as Samuel did and respond in faith when God speaks: "Speak, Lord, for your servant listens." Humbly submit yourself to listen to the Lord and respond in obedience to what He says.

Go Deeper

- Do you have any long-held beliefs from your church past that may be hindering you from hearing God speak? How can you get past this?

- Can you remember a prayer that changed your life? Think about it and write down how God answered that prayer.

- Did you recognize the answer at the time or later?

- Read Joel 2:28–29; Acts 2:17–18; Hebrews 11:8.

- How do these Scriptures support or contradict your answer to the question above?

Activation Prayer

Lord, I want to know You more. Help me discern Your truth and awaken me to the ways You speak. Tune my heart to hear Your voice. I do not want to miss when You speak to me. Help me to be like Samuel and respond in faith when I sense You are speaking to me.

Activate Encouragement

If we are not aware that God is speaking all the time, then we can easily miss it when He does. God will often bump up against our lives with Scriptures, thoughts, impressions, pictures, a single word or a phrase. Let's begin to pay attention to the things around us and start noting little things like:

- Scriptures that jump off the page when you read the Word
- Someone's name popping into your mind at random times
- Random songs or lyrics running through your mind
- Things that catch your attention in your daily life, such as objects in nature (e.g., a sunrise/sunset, an animal or a specific color)

Once you note them, then take it a step further and ask God: "God, are You trying to tell me something in what I am reading, hearing or seeing?"

If someone's name randomly comes to mind, ask God: "Is there a reason I am thinking of him or her? Do I need to pray for this person? Give this person a call? Or do something else?"

Like Samuel, we need to respond in faith to what could be God bumping into our everyday routine. When we ask the question, "God, is that You?" be ready for Him to respond.

Think on It!

Relationship Revelation

God wants to have a deeper relationship with each one of us. He desires that we live out the spiritual gift of prophecy. This begins with the ability to hear Him.

The Lord spoke one simple sentence to me that changed everything: *The prophetic is all about relationship!* I had no clue what this meant, but I obediently wrote it down. I knew God was not going to speak something to me only to leave me hanging. I earnestly began to seek Him more.

Yet as I sat at His feet, I felt like I was plowing concrete. When I tried to pray for any period of time, my mind would wander and the slightest distraction would capture me, such as, *Did I put the clothes in the dryer?*

To say this was hard is an understatement. It was torture. God was asking me to grow our relationship, to be brave and to go deeper. He was no longer content with me staying on the surface. He wanted me to learn how to be with Him and experience the depth of His love. At times I still struggle, but then I remember God is not after my perfection; He's after my obedience.

Activation Prayer

Father God, show me what I need to do to grow my relationship with You. Help me set aside any desire or need to be perfect. Instead, I yield myself to You and allow You to perfect me. Lord, help me to be obedient when You speak and allow me to experience a new depth of Your love today.

Go Deeper

- When you hear someone speak about the gift of prophecy, what do you think?

- What do you think it means to hear from God?

- God asks all of us to grow our relationship with Him. For you, what might that look like? And what might He want you to do?

4

A Glimpse of the Prophetic

When my youngest child was ready for kindergarten I was offered an administrative position in the worship arts department
of our church. In our church the term *worship* meant music and
all the techy stuff (sound, lighting and video) that went into
making a service happen. It is important to know this because
I am not musically or technically gifted at all! Working for the
worship department seemed like a really odd fit. As it turned
out, I was exactly what they were looking for.

Several months into the job, our pastor announced that a
special prophetic guest was coming to speak. I had no clue
what the prophetic was about, but everyone on staff was excited. We were told our guest would be ministering during our
Wednesday-night service, and some of the staff made plans to
get seats right in the front. It sounds funny now, but I really
wanted to receive ministry, so I decided to wear my brightest
colored suit jacket in order to stand out.

When the evening came I arrived early and settled in the front
row. Our speaker shared her message and then explained about
the prophetic and how it operated in her life. She took a minute

to pray and asked the Lord to speak to her. She then walked back and forth on the platform, looking out into the audience. As she ministered, she would stop and speak to various individuals. As she spoke prophetic words over people, I thought, *How can a person hear the Lord speak to her for someone else? Can this really be the Lord?*

Our guest speaker tried to demystify her ministering as much as she could, but I was completely in awe of what was happening. It was as if something inside of me was awakening. At one point she asked all staff members to stand up. My heart was racing. *Here it is. Finally, I'm going to be chosen! I'll be given a word.* A thought crossed my mind: *What if it's embarrassing? Do I really want all these people to know what God has to say about me?* She thanked us for standing up and explained she would not be giving words to any of us that night because she would be ministering to us the following day. *Rats.* How was I supposed to get any sleep?

The next morning as we all gathered I listened to the powerful words being shared over the pastors and staff. We were a large group, so I knew it would take a while for her to get to me. Finally, it was my turn. The lady sitting right beside me received a terrific word, and I anticipated the same wow factor. This is the transcript of the prophetic word spoken over me that morning.

> I see a song in you. Do you sing? No? Okay, this is the kind of song I see in you. It's a great capacity to love. You want to sing this love song to God just as loud as you can possibly sing. You just want to sing to God and tell Him how wonderful He is. It doesn't even matter if it is on key. You have a huge capacity to love God. I want to pray to free it up to flow to its fullest. Father, there is such a huge capacity within her to love You, to have a wild love affair with You, and I ask that You free her up to flow in the depths of that love, in Jesus' name.
>
> I see lifeless little babies in front of you. I think those are dreams, visions and hopes that you have never allowed or think

could not come to pass. I speak to each one of them, and I say, "Live, in the name of Jesus. Live, in the name of Jesus. Live, in the name of Jesus. Live, in the name of Jesus." I command them to come to life and live, in Jesus' name. I call them forth to live in Jesus' name, in Jesus' name, in Jesus' name!

You have the potential. Now, it will take a while for Jesus to develop it within you. You know how the pendulum will swing way over here and then way over there, and then it gets in the middle? You have this bottled-up desire to be a blessing, and as you start blessing God—I mean get up every day and start blessing Him; sing love songs to Him at the top of your voice; it doesn't matter if you are any good at it; just start loving God—what will happen is you'll really flow in that. Then you'll swing over here and love people. Then you'll get right here in the middle where you are able to walk it out and put the two together.

You have such a capacity in there, honey, and these dreams that you've never allowed to come to life because you thought you could never have them—that is a lie from the pit of hell. You can have them. You can walk in them, and you can be extremely good at what you do. So I call it forth in the name of Jesus.

Now, I know this is going to sound ungrateful, but my first thought was, *That's it?* I mean, really? This word took less than a minute to give. I can see the importance of the word now, but back then it felt like everyone else received impressive, spiritual words. The lady next to me received a word about being a tall tree planted beside the river, able to drink deeply in the things of the Lord. I wanted a word like hers! I was seriously disappointed.

Have you ever been so excited to receive ministry or prayer, only to be left disappointed? I know I am not the only one ever to have had such an experience. Remember the woman I met at a conference who confessed to stalking me on Facebook? As soon as I finished ministering to her and her friend she joked about not getting a "cool word" like her friend. The word I gave to her friend was about God creating a masterpiece for her with one single stroke; she was being given a crown she had been eyeing, and God told her to dream bigger. It was an awesome word. I would have wanted it too.

I knew she was disappointed with the word she received; yet at the same time, God's message was not flowery or "cool," but it was specific to current and past events in her life.* God gave me two separate pictures, but it was the second one that was the most impactful to us both.

I saw a picture of toast with jam spread on it, and a finger drawing a happy face in the jam. I had no idea what to do with this picture and asked if it meant something to her. She acknowledged it did. She was emotional, but that's all the confirmation I got. I told her I felt God was pointing to a specific event in her life, and He wanted her to know that He saw her and He knew. When I had finished she asked if she could talk with me before the next session. I agreed but was not expecting the following conversation. As we walked, she confided the following story to me:

> The picture of the toast is a moment from my past. When I was eight or nine my abusive stepdad forced me to eat things I literally couldn't eat because they caused me to gag and throw up. Jam was one of those foods. Sometimes I would be forced to sit in a chair for hours and even days until I'd eat it or, more usually, get a beating. One particular time at breakfast I was having toast with just butter when my stepdad decided he was going to "cure" me of my jam issue. He spread a massively thick layer on a piece of toast, and I was literally unable to eat it. I sat there for two days, not even being allowed to go to the bathroom or to my room to sleep, or have any additional food or drink. Though I had no exposure to God at all in my

---

*This is a word of knowledge. See appendix 1.

childhood, there was this one beautiful moment as I sat in front of that toast in which I became fully aware that this man was a monster, and I was not his. It was as if God was calling me to Himself even then. I felt a sudden peace and joy and, I guess, a sudden sense of resolve. I may have to endure this man for a long time, I thought, but I wouldn't have to forever. I belonged to someone else. I belonged to God. So I made a smiley face in the jam with my finger that day. It resulted in a broken bone, but if I remember correctly, I think this was the last time one of those food episodes took place.

I listened as she shared her story. I hurt for what she had endured as a little child and yet felt blessed to have the opportunity to speak a word of healing and comfort. There was never a situation where she was alone. God was calling her to Himself, despite how she felt about the spoken word. God gives us what we need in the moment, even if we do not recognize it as such.

Now, back to the rest of my story. Once our special guest was finished, it was the staff's turn to minister to her. She encouraged us to share whatever was brought to our minds. This might be a picture, a word, an impression or a combination of all three. If we didn't know what it meant, she would help us with the interpretation. As we gathered around her I saw a picture in my mind. I was amazed and a little afraid. I had never spoken up in a group before, much less a group of pastors. I was hesitant to open my mouth, but I felt compelled to share. This is the word picture I gave:

I saw an old-fashioned pitcher and washbasin, the kind that were used before indoor plumbing and running water. The pitcher and the bowl were sitting there like a still photograph. As I continued to watch the picture it became animated, and I saw liquid from the pitcher pouring into the bowl. The bowl represented other people and ministries she would pour into. She was constantly pouring out. It came to the point, however, where there wasn't anything left to pour. Then I saw the hand of the Lord come down, take the pitcher and set it into the basin of the bowl, so that it rested in its proper position. Then I saw water being poured out from heaven into the pitcher, and the pitcher began to fill up with water and overflow.

This is the first time I remember being purposeful about receiving and delivering a word from God. After I finished, I slowly sank back into my seat. I could feel my entire body shaking from the adrenaline of stepping out to minister. Little did I know this shaking can be a physical response to the Holy Spirit empowering us to minister. I knew something very important had happened. God was finally showing me the calling He had placed on my life.

Was this really prophecy?

Following a women's retreat where I spoke, I was ministering to a young woman who suffered severe back pain resulting from a car accident. A teenage girl with the retreat tech team shared this story with me.

I needed prayer for things I was going through, but since I was serving, I couldn't go get prayer. I felt stuck, which made me grumpy. I determined when the song was over I would go get prayer, but as I glanced up to see Debbie praying over a woman, I felt God prompt me to pray for the woman's healing. I proceeded to push the thought out of my head and even said, "God, if that's You, I don't want to. I need prayer myself." I could see in the natural she was using a cane to walk, so I figured the healing part was right. But the Lord kept prompting me to pray for this woman's healing. Finally, I relented and approached her when the program ended. When I first prayed for her healing I felt the Lord say, "Keep praying until she's healed." I did just that. After twenty minutes or so of praying and testing the measure of her healing, God touched her and healed her back pain completely. She could walk without using her cane from then on. I was completely in awe and blessed that God would use me in this way. As I prayed over the woman my heart and attitude changed, and I received ministry from the Lord too while participating in praying for her. Even more exciting was how she was impacted from the touch of God on her life. She rededicated her life fully to God and was even baptized the following year at retreat.

Have you felt the prompting of the Lord to pray for someone but did not want to? Or you didn't know what to pray? Maybe you felt God nudging you to say something to someone, but you had no way of knowing if it was right or not? Maybe you had a bad attitude or even a "me first" mentality.

Proverbs 11:25 assures us, "A generous person will prosper; whoever refreshes others will be refreshed." I can promise you, you will not always know it is right until you step out in faith to do the very thing you feel God is prompting you to do. When you do He will give you the words to speak and show you the things to do, just like He did for me and just like He did for the young teenage girl with the grumpy attitude. God wants us to encourage one another. We do this by listening to the prompting of His voice in our heart and mind.

Go Deeper

- Read 1 Corinthians 14:1–5, 31. Who do these verses say should be operating in prophecy?

- What is the purpose of prophecy?

- Have you ever received a prophetic word or word of encouragement from someone? How did it affect you?

Activation Prayer

Jesus, I want to have a heart to love and encourage people like You modeled throughout Scripture. Allow me to be used by You to bring encouragement to others, even when I feel I need it myself. Lord, help me to step out past fear and emotions and respond to what I feel You are asking me to do. Use me to be a blessing and encouragement to people today.

Activate Encouragement

As you go about your day, if a person's name crosses your mind, write it down. Now, ask God to give you a specific Scripture you can share to encourage that person.

Think on It!

God Wants You!

Have you ever wondered why God wants us? Why would God choose to use you or me as a part of His plans and purposes when it seems there are more "spiritually qualified" people in the world? Have you ever tried to disqualify yourself?

"God could never use me because _____" (fill in the blank).

> But God chose the foolish things of the world to shame the wise; God chose the weak things of the world to shame the strong.
>
> 1 Corinthians 1:27

In this verse, Paul was telling the church in Corinth they were not disqualified because they lacked an education. Before Paul was "Paul the apostle" he was Saul, a legalistic theologian, a murderer of Christians and an enemy of God. God did not disqualify Paul because of his past, and God does not disqualify you!

God knew us before the foundations of the world. He does not need our help to accomplish anything. He is God. Yet He longs for relationship and partnership with us so we can experience "on earth as it is in heaven."

His Ability + His Power + His Anointing + You = The Extraordinary

Activation Prayer

Lord Jesus, I repent and ask forgiveness for times I may have disqualified myself from serving You. God, I believe You have a plan and a purpose for my life, and I choose to trust You. Help me to partner with You and Your Holy Spirit.

Go Deeper

- *God wants you!* What is your initial reaction to reading those words?

- Do you think God would choose you for a special task?

- Have you ever disqualified yourself from serving God? If so, how and why?

- Read 1 Corinthians 1:27. How does this verse specifically apply in your life?

5

Chosen and Qualified

I was hungry to learn what the Scriptures actually taught about the prophetic. When I received an invitation to attend prophetic classes I jumped at the chance. Deep down I believed hearing from God was for people more spiritual than I. I didn't know exactly what this meant. I flat-out did not feel qualified. I was on a yo-yo between firm belief and confusion and doubt.

As the weeks passed, my classmates encouraged me and told me I was right on track with the words I was getting, but I just felt they were only being nice. I did not doubt God could speak to His children; I doubted He would speak through me.

Soon after the classes ended I received a call asking me to be a part of a prophetic team at an upcoming church event. I was surprised and flattered but confused. If these folks were really discerning of gifts, why would they choose me? I certainly did not feel as though I had a prophetic gifting. During the drive to the event I prayed that God would help me out of this mess. I was bombarded with doubt and insecurity.

When the first person approached us for ministry I knowingly smiled at my partner to begin. When it was my turn I agreed with what was spoken and blessed the individual in Jesus' name. I felt like a complete fraud.

At one point, as a woman stood waiting for a word, my partner turned to me and said, "I think you should go first." She tried to hand me the tape recorder, and I stared at it. I did not reach for it and mumbled that I didn't have anything yet. My partner looked at me, smiled and replied, "That's okay. We can wait. God will give you something." I began praying earnestly. Almost immediately I saw a picture. Papers were stacked high on a desk in piles of varying heights. I sensed the lady was overwhelmed by her job. When I shared this picture and my impression, she seemed really upset. She looked me straight in the eye and asked, "My husband came to you and told you what's going on, didn't he?" I assured her I did not know who she was and proceeded to share the rest of what God showed me. She grew more and more upset in spite of my assurances. It was obvious she did not believe me. She walked away visibly angry, and I wanted to sink into the floor.

As I prepared to leave, the lady approached me and asked if we could talk. She seemed a bit embarrassed. She was the church's administrative pastor and was feeling completely overwhelmed and overworked. It had gotten so bad she considered quitting. When I described the piles of paper work that were literally sitting on her desk, she genuinely believed her husband had spoken with me. After she took a few minutes to calm down and pray, she knew God was speaking to her. I was stunned.

Looking back, even though I heard correctly, I did not know what I was doing. But I cooperated with God, and He always knows what He is doing.

I disqualified myself because I did not fully understand God's nature. I was focusing on my shortcomings, but He knew my areas of strength and my potential. God wanted to perfect me; He did not want me to be perfect.

Have you ever been asked to step out in an area of ministry yet felt completely unqualified and, worse, not called? You are not the only one who has felt this way, as evidenced by the following stories.

Vonda, the assistant women's ministry director at her church, has a desire to help women realize they are strong, passionate and creative. She believes when women work together they are unstoppable. Recently, she was asked to speak at her church's women's retreat. Yet Vonda felt unqualified despite wanting the opportunity to minister. Planning fun events and bringing women together around activities was one thing, but to be a speaker during a retreat, well, that was completely different. She felt like a complete fraud and felt she did not have anything of value to share with the women. But she said yes anyway.

After the retreat, women shared with Vonda how her message helped to set the tone for an entire weekend of God ministering and women being set free. One simple yes on her part by stepping forward in obedience was met by God. He always knows what He is doing. Even when we feel unqualified or like a fraud, God knows we can do it. He chose us; we simply need to respond and trust Him.

Denise also shared her story with me about feeling unqualified. Denise was scared to death and trembling with anxiety the first time she was called on to give an encouraging word during prophetic training. She was bombarded with many thoughts, like, *What if I don't get anything? What if God doesn't come through for me?* She was certain everyone else around her had a direct pipeline to hear God's voice and she was going to be the only one who did not hear Him. Fast forward two years later. Denise shared with me how she still gets incredibly nervous, but she can honestly say God has come through for her even when she doubts.

Denise recalled recently needing to give encouragement to someone, but she agonized over it. "Oh please, oh please, let me get something," she prayed under her breath. Then it came: a picture of an octopus. *Um, no. No, God, I don't think that is it. It doesn't feel spiritual enough. They're going to think this is weird.* While she was disputing the fact that a picture of an octopus could be from God, she began to rationalize and asked God for anything else.

She waited. She prayed some more. But nothing came. *Ugh.* Denise took a deep breath and thought, *Okay, here goes.* As she shared the picture, the woman lit up. Denise shared how she felt God was saying the woman took on too much and had her hands in too many things. The woman confirmed she had recently been told this by church leaders. Denise's word was confirmation. Denise says even though sharing a prophetic word is sometimes scary and nerve-wracking, she breathes in deeply and remembers the octopus picture. When she does this it makes all the difference in her faith. Now she knows God speaks to her and He can use her to be an encouragement to others.

In case you are still feeling disqualified, don't forget about the exhaustive list of biblical giants whose great feats of faith are shared along with their shortcomings. In the Old Testament we read about how Noah once got so drunk that he wound up naked and in need of covering. Jacob lied and manipulated his brother in order to steal Esau's blessing from their father. Moses had a stuttering problem, Rahab was a prostitute, and David committed both adultery and murder. In the New Testament, Christ's own disciples fell asleep when He needed them most, and then Peter denied Christ three times. Martha was a worrier. Paul, before his conversion, even murdered Christians in his religious zeal. And yet, God used each of these men and women and saw fit to include their stories of faith in His Word.

Go Deeper

- Do you feel chosen by God?

- Do you think your name could ever be listed alongside God's faith-filled giants? (See the list in Hebrews 11.) If not, why? What does God's Word say about your potential for faith and who you are in Him?

- Reread the list of biblical figures in the last full paragraph above the Go Deeper section. To whom do you most relate? Why?

- Do you believe God has chosen you? Why or why not?

Activation Prayer

Lord Jesus, at times I feel disqualified or like a complete failure because of my incorrect view of myself. Jesus, help me not only to know in my head but also to believe with all my heart that You have chosen me. God, I lay aside my desire to be perfect and ask that You would perfect me. Thank You for not disqualifying me because of anything I have done in the past. Thank You for being a God of forgiveness, love and multiple chances. I gladly say yes to being chosen by You, God. Here I am; show me what You have chosen for me to do.

Activate Encouragement

Ask God for a specific Scripture that speaks to your identity in Christ. It will be a verse or passage you can hold on to and proclaim over yourself at times when you feel less than or when feelings of being inadequate overwhelm you. Once God gives you this verse or passage, write it out, memorize it, speak it out loud daily and put it in a place where you will see it often.

6

Prophecy 101

The words *prophecy* and *prophet* are buzzwords that cause many to be uncomfortable. Too many believers become hopelessly ensnared by questions like, What is prophecy? Is it even biblical? Is it for today?

Yes, it is for today and, yes, it is biblical. Instead of focusing on buzzwords, let's focus on Jesus' lifestyle of prophetic encouragement. The gift of prophecy always has the heart of God behind it, which is love! (See 1 Corinthians 13:1–7.)

Several examples have been given already regarding the prophetic. In this chapter I want to give you a solid foundation before continuing. Oftentimes when people hear the word *prophecy,* they look to Old Testament examples and get their definition from that alone, but there is much more to consider.

Prophecy by definition is calling forth and declaring God's plans or the speaking of future events. This is what we read about in the Old Testament. Since Jesus' death, resurrection and ascension, prophecy has taken on a much more personal purpose. In the New Testament Paul discusses the gift of prophecy (see 1 Corinthians 14:1–5) as something for all, giving prophecy a new definition. Prophecy's purpose is to strengthen, encourage and comfort those who hear and receive it. Today when people operate in the spiritual gift of prophecy it is often in harmony with a word of wisdom or a word of knowledge. (See appendix 1 for more on both prophecy and words of knowledge.)

Four Purposes of Prophecy

Did you know there are four major purposes for prophecy? If you didn't, you are not alone.

1. For strengthening or edification; encouragement or exhortation; comfort (see 1 Corinthians 14:3–4)

   a. *Strengthening or edification*: to build up

   b. *Encouragement or exhortation*: to call near, impart hope, build confidence; to put courage into someone

   c. *Comfort*: "to soothe, console, or reassure; to cheer up"*

2. To reveal the secrets of people's hearts (see 1 Corinthians 14:24–25)

   a. God does not reveal the secrets of a person's heart to embarrass him or her but rather to convince an unbeliever He is real.

   b. Prophecy can soften and change a person's heart.

3. To bring to pass what God has spoken (see Genesis 41; 49; Daniel 2; Isaiah 7:14; Jeremiah 23:5; 49:16; Ezekiel 29:15; 37; Micah 5:1–2; Matthew 24:29–31, 36–37; 2 Peter 3:1–18; 1 Thessalonians 5:1–9; Revelation 1–22)

   a. God spoke through His prophets in the Old Testament to foretell what was to come.

   b. These messages were also intended to share God's plan with His people.

*Definition of *comfort* quoted from Dictionary.com.

4. To move God's people into obedience

    a. Throughout the Old Testament God uses the phrase "be careful to obey" (see Leviticus 25:18; Deuteronomy 6:3; Joshua 1:7).

    b. God's messages to His people were meant to correct and reconcile them back to Him.

    c. Obedience is an important element in hearing God.

Four Levels of the Prophetic

There is also confusion about how, when and why the Holy Spirit moves here on earth. This comes from a lack of understanding regarding the four purposes and four distinct levels outlined in Scripture. One layer (level) of the prophetic is not more important than the other. They are:

1. Prophetic atmosphere/environment
2. Spiritual gift of prophecy
3. Mantle of the prophetic
4. The office of prophet

Prophetic Environment

When the Holy Spirit is given room to flow, people who have never moved in the gift of prophecy are able to prophesy. A prophetic environment can take place when a prophetically anointed individual, in cooperation with the Holy Spirit, creates an atmosphere that allows others to step under their umbrella of anointing.

In 1 Samuel we see the power of a prophetically charged atmosphere.

But when they saw a group of prophets prophesying, with Samuel standing there as their leader, the Spirit of God came on Saul's men, and they also prophesied. Saul was told about it, and he sent more men, and they prophesied too. Saul sent men a third time, and they also prophesied. . . . So Saul went to Naioth at Ramah. But the Spirit of God came even on him, and he walked along prophesying until he came to Naioth. He stripped off his garments, and he too prophesied in Samuel's presence. He lay naked all that day and all that night. This is why people say, "Is Saul also among the prophets?"

1 Samuel 19:20–21, 23–24

Is Saul among the prophets? No, but when the atmosphere is charged, the Holy Spirit can disburse gifts as He wills, and ordinary people such as Saul can prophesy.

Spiritual Gift of Prophecy

There are nine different spiritual gifts given solely by the prompting of the Holy Spirit. Prophecy is one of these gifts. They are given for the edification of the Church, the body of Christ. God longs for the prophetic to be understood and used by all.

There are different kinds of gifts, but the same Spirit distributes them. There are different kinds of service, but the same Lord. There are different kinds of working, but in all of them and in everyone it is the same God at work. Now to each one the manifestation of the Spirit is given for the common good. To one there is given through the Spirit a *message of wisdom*, to another a *message of knowledge* by means of the same Spirit, to another *faith* by the same Spirit, to another *gifts of healing* by that one Spirit, to another *miraculous powers*, to another *prophecy*, to another *distinguishing between spirits*, to another *speaking in different kinds of tongues*, and to still another the *interpretation of tongues*. All these are the work of one and the same Spirit, and he distributes them to each one, just as he determines.

1 Corinthians 12:4–11, emphasis added

Paul tells us all that we should desire all the spiritual gifts but especially the gift of prophecy. Why is the gift of prophecy so important? Paul tells us it is to strengthen, encourage and edify one another.

> Follow the way of love and eagerly desire gifts of the Spirit, especially prophecy. For anyone who speaks in a tongue does not speak to people but to God. Indeed, no one understands them; they utter mysteries by the Spirit. But the one who prophesies speaks to people for their strengthening, encouraging and comfort. Anyone who speaks in a tongue edifies themselves, but the one who prophesies edifies the church. I would like every one of you to speak in tongues, *but I would rather have you prophesy.*
>
> 1 Corinthians 14:1–5, emphasis added

The gift of prophecy (hearing the words of God for others) is for everyone! We are to desire all the gifts, which means anyone can operate and function in any of the gifts as the need arises.

Mantle of the Prophetic

God can bestow a specific gift of prophecy, which entails an increased ability to hear Him. This gift is called the mantle of the prophetic. It is a supernatural anointing given to individuals to operate at an intimate level within the spiritual gift of prophecy. People who have this gifting often operate in two areas of the prophetic: foretelling (of future events) and forth-telling (calling forth situations or circumstances).

This gift is evident by the fruit of their life.

> The Spirit of the Sovereign LORD is on me, because *the LORD has anointed* me to proclaim good news to the poor.
>
> Isaiah 61:1, emphasis added

People who operate in this gift have a more heightened level than those experiencing a prophetic atmosphere and those activating the basic spiritual gift of prophecy. In other words, it is a stronger, more powerful version of the basic spiritual gift of the prophetic. Furthermore, their ministry tends to be marked by accuracy and life-giving words.

> As each one has received a special gift, employ it in serving one another as good stewards of the manifold grace of God.
>
> 1 Peter 4:10 NASB

Someone with this level of anointing can and should be operating in this gift continuously. These anointed individuals are not prophets, though, because they have not received a calling to the office of prophet.

The Office of Prophet

Biblically, to be a prophet is a calling from God, and the prophet fulfills the office, or role, of a prophet. This is a job description. Just because you can prophesy, it does not mean you are a prophet, nor does it mean you carry a mantle for the prophetic.

> And he gave the *apostles, the prophets, the evangelists, the shepherds and teachers*, to equip the saints for the work of ministry, for building up the body of Christ.
>
> Ephesians 4:11–12 ESV, emphasis added

A person who bears the title *prophet* has the gift of prophecy for the purpose of teaching others. If you are called to the office of prophet, your job is to equip God's people for the work of ministry. This is one of the God-appointed, fivefold offices.

Take Jeremiah for example. The Lord told him:

72

Before I formed you in the womb I knew you, and before you were born I consecrated you; I appointed you a prophet to the nations.

Jeremiah 1:5 ESV

A prophet's assignment is to hear God and release this to the people. In looking at the four levels of the prophetic, the office of prophet is a position of authority not because of who the prophet is but because of the anointing God placed on the office.

The prophet is not more important than everyone else. We all have equal value as members of the body. We need all of the parts working and functioning together.

Just as each of us has one body with many members, and these members do not all have the same function, so in Christ we, though many, form one body, and each member belongs to all the others. *We have different gifts, according to the grace given to each of us.* If your gift is prophesying, then prophesy in accordance with your faith; if it is serving, then serve. . . . Love must be sincere.

Romans 12:4–7, 9, emphasis added

In the church we look to the person standing behind the pulpit every week as the person in charge. Do the people within the congregation look at that individual as more important than themselves? *Long pause.* The answer should be no.

According to God, a pastor is no more important than anyone else in the congregation. Do not confuse the responsibility or accountability God places upon a pastor with his or her value as a person. We may view a pastor or prophet as being superior, but neither being a pastor nor being a prophet means he or she is a super Christian. The biblical truth is that their gifting does not increase their importance within the body, only their accountability (see James 3:1).

We should never be focused on the gifting of one person; instead, we should be focused on the One who has bestowed that gift upon them, Jesus Christ.

Go Deeper

- What are the four levels of the prophetic?

- In 1 Corinthians 14:1–5, why does Paul tell us we should desire the gift of prophecy?

- Do you think one gift is more important than another? Why or why not? What Scripture supports your answer?

Activation Prayer

God, help me to honor those You have placed in a position of responsibility within the body of Christ. God, show me if I have focused on a person or a gifting instead of focusing on You. If I have, please forgive me for doing so and help me step out more in the gift of prophetic encouragement.

Activate Encouragement

Choose someone in your life who needs a word of encouragement. Write the name down in your journal, on a note card or on a piece of paper.

Purposefully pray and ask God to share a Scripture, a sentence or a thought that you can share with the person. Write down whatever God brings to your mind and heart. After you have written the encouraging word down, make time to call or meet the person face-to-face to share the encouragement God has specifically given you for them.

Think on It!

The Holy Spirit

The Holy Spirit, the third Person in the Trinity, is just as essential as God and His Son, Jesus. Still, the Holy Spirit is often overlooked or not addressed in some churches today because some of His gifts are considered controversial and are often misunderstood. Such was the case in the church where I was raised. Once I received some solid teaching,* I fully embraced the Holy Spirit in my life. The following terminology helped me to understand better what the Holy Spirit's job is. The Holy Spirit is to be:

- With us—Before we are saved the Holy Spirit draws us to Jesus (see John 14:16).
- Within us—This happens at the moment of salvation (see John 14:17).
- Upon us—This happens after the "within us" experience but is separate and in addition to our salvation experience. It is when we receive power (see Acts 8:15, 18; 10:44–47; 19:6; Revelation 3:20).

The Holy Spirit is given to us as a gift (see Luke 24:49; Acts 1:4–8). He is an essential part of living life the way God intended. The Holy Spirit is key to experiencing a supernatural lifestyle and walking in the gift of prophetic encouragement. God in His infinite wisdom knew we would need a Helper to live our life once Jesus went back to heaven (see John 15:26; 16:5–14). The Holy Spirit is God's gift to us. It is a free gift, should we choose to receive it.

In fact, I believe it is not a suggestion but a command that we ask for the Holy Spirit to come live within us and be upon us, clothing us with His power from on high. The Holy Spirit is described as rivers of living water (see John 7:37–39) and brings with Himself the ability to walk in the fruit (see Galatians 5:22–23) and the gifts (see 1 Corinthians 12:4–11) of the Holy Spirit. We all need the "upon us" experience, and it happens the moment we ask. We also need

*The teaching I received was from John and Sonja Decker's Ministry Training Institute and their training book, *Kingdom Living*.

to ask for a fresh, new overflowing and infilling of His Spirit daily (see Lamentations 3:22–24).

> Then Peter stood up with the Eleven, raised his voice and addressed the crowd. . . . "This is what was spoken by the prophet Joel: 'In the last days, God says, I will pour out my Spirit on all people. Your sons and daughters will prophesy, your young men will see visions, your old men will dream dreams. Even on my servants, both men and women, I will pour out my Spirit in those days, and they will prophesy. I will show wonders in the heavens above and signs on the earth below, blood and fire and billows of smoke. The sun will be turned to darkness and the moon to blood before the coming of the great and glorious day of the Lord. And everyone who calls on the name of the Lord will be saved.'"
>
> Acts 2:14–21

(If you have not prayed to receive the Holy Spirit baptism, turn to appendix 3 and follow the steps to receive this free gift.)

Activation Prayer

Lord, open me up to Your truths found in the Word of God regarding the Holy Spirit baptism. God, I want to live a powerful, effective life for the Kingdom of God, and I know that I cannot do it of my own accord. I need You. Would You send Your Spirit to equip me and clothe me daily with power from on high to accomplish the work You have for me to do here on earth? Thank You for this free gift and for Your Holy Spirit.

Go Deeper

- What are your beliefs on the baptism of the Holy Spirit?

- Read Acts 2. As you read this chapter, what stands out to you regarding the Holy Spirit?

- Do you feel Acts 2:14–21 applies to us today, or are we still waiting for this to occur? Why or why not?

7

First Steps

I used to say that if God was going to speak to me, He'd better take out a billboard telling me to make a right turn five miles ahead and then have a flashing neon sign saying, "You have arrived!" The truth is, God speaks to us, and we often miss it because we are expecting the iconic, booming James Earl Jones voice to grab our attention. Most of the time God's voice is not what we expect. God speaks in a variety of ways: through His Word, through other people and even through our own thoughts. These things are so familiar to us we often discount them. As we begin to listen and hear God we must trust the Holy Spirit and have faith to believe what we are hearing and experiencing.

When I first began to grasp that God speaks today and He was speaking to me, I was grateful to have a prophetic "recipe." I was taught in order to minister you simply needed to follow the instructions, and you would hear from God. The not-so-subtle implication was that if I followed the recipe and I did not hear from God, I was doing something wrong. I had a hard time believing I was not making it up in my own mind.

As I grow deeper in my relationship with God He is faithful in helping me to recognize His voice. We are all different, and God speaks to each one of us in a unique way. There is no one recipe to hear from God.

One of the best ways to activate your ability to hear God is to read the Bible, which is a primary way He speaks. When someone tells me that they cannot hear from God, I assign Scripture reading and ask them to pray, read and write down the verse that stands out to them and why. I then encourage them to share it with someone. It is truly astounding how unique and personal the message is! Any time God speaks it will always line up with the Bible. As you read the Bible and are quickened to a particular verse or passage, recognize God is speaking. Take time to go deeper and ask Him questions. He is always faithful to speak.

Scripture is full of examples of different ways in which God speaks. One of my favorites is when God spoke through a donkey (see Numbers 22). Here is a short list containing a few examples of ways God can communicate with us.

• The Bible	• Visions	• Events
• A word	• Angels	• Books
• Pictures	• Nature	• Other people
• Impressions	• Music	• Sermons
• Sounds	• Songs	• Journaling
• Audible voices	• Movies	
• Dreams	• Thoughts	

Since the Bible is a primary way God speaks, we need to begin to read it with a fresh new perspective. As we read Scripture, remember you are not just reading it for yourself; you are reading to impart to others. Ask God to give you eyes to see and a heart to know when others may need to be encouraged by a particular verse, story or concept found in the pages of Scripture. I have often found that when I am reading God's Word and He shows me a revelation or gives me personal encouragement, I am soon presented with opportunities to share or encourage others with what He just showed me.

Do you ever wonder if you are hearing from God or making things up in your own mind? When the Gilbaugh family first took my classes they wondered if God was really speaking to them. They shared with me the skepticism and apprehension they felt prior to and even during the training. Tiffany wrote:

> Growing up a preacher's kid I thought I knew what "hearing from God" was all about. Little did I know that I really knew very little! Before Debbie's class, I had a very narrow and fuzzy picture of what God can and will do to speak to us. Now I feel as though my vision has been made clear. I can see how God will speak to me in my everyday surroundings as well as my time in His Word. But the blessing has not just been for me. My children (then ages six and ten) amaze me every day with the way they will stop and pray to find something they are missing or to encourage a friend. My husband now can "let go and let God" because he has learned to hear His voice. Once restrictive with giving, we are now blessing missionaries in Africa out of obedience to God.
>
> To me, that is what hearing from God is all about: When we hear from Him, we can build up, bless and encourage others with His love! My eyes opened to fully see Him!

Tiffany's husband, Mark, shared how learning to hear from God changed his life:

> After two tours to Iraq as a medivac instructor pilot I had only been home for five months in two and a half years between training and deployments. As a result, my family and my mental health were suffering. Iraq was a spiritually oppressed land, and the weight of that spiritual battle weighed heavily on me. I had seen enough human carnage and mutilation to last a hundred lifetimes.

In 2006 I was honorably discharged from the Army and started a small telecommunications company soon thereafter. By 2010 we had run out of money, our family had lost our business, and we were forced to file for personal bankruptcy. Our creditors refused to work with us any longer, and attorneys for these financial institutions were starting to contact us about forthcoming lawsuits. We lost our house and cars in the process, and God was preparing us to start over. As the leader of our home, I was in a desperate place. I needed God's direction.

A friend from church invited us to Debbie's training, and it was exactly what I needed. I had not really experienced the gifts of the Spirit, but I believed they were real. I believed our loving Creator would want to communicate with us if we could filter out the world's noise for a few minutes.

During the training exercises we would pray and ask God for prophetic messages. At first my mind would wander and I struggled to filter out the random conversations from the day. Now I am able to discern the voice of God sooner.

When the Gilbaughs gave me permission to share their testimonies, Mark wrote one line attached to his email: "Thanks for changing our family tree and direction! You made an impact and left a legacy in us!" This is my heart's cry and prayer for everyone. It also demonstrates the power of the prophetic to encourage and transform lives.

The prophetic gift of encouragement is about making a difference and impacting individuals in a way you may never have thought possible. It is about giving people tools to help them impact others, and in turn they are changed for the better. When we encourage others, we literally put courage into them.

God wants us to encourage each other and move in the spiritual gift of prophecy, but our direct relationship with Him must come first. His voice—prophecy flowing through us—comes after this. It is out of the overflow of our relationship with Him that we develop a deep and genuine love to share God's heart with others.

Through a relationship with Him we gain the confidence and knowledge to prophesy. We are tuned to His voice as we strengthen the bond of our relationship with Him: "My sheep hear my voice, and I know them, and they follow me" (John 10:27 ESV).

Go Deeper

- Read Job 33:14. What does this verse say about the way God speaks?

- Reading the Bible is a primary way God speaks to His people. How can you incorporate the Scriptures into your daily conversations as the Holy Spirit leads?

- After reading the list of ways God communicates with His people, did you realize that God has spoken to you without your realizing it?

Activation Prayer

God, I want to hear from You. Help me recognize when You are speaking to me. Let me not compare myself to others or look for You to speak the same way You do to others, because You have made me unique. Your Word promises that because I am one of Your children I will hear Your voice and follow after You. Open my spiritual eyes and ears to see and hear Your heart for me and for others. Help me to find the ways You communicate with me so that I may encourage others.

Activate Encouragement

Before we can expect God to speak His words of encouragement through us, we must be able to recognize and discern when He is speaking. Maybe you feel you have never experienced the Lord speaking to you personally, but the truth is, He is always speaking.

For this activation, read Psalm 23 in its entirety. As you read, pay attention and jot down any verse or phrase that stands out to you. Once you have done this, ask the Lord if there is specific significance for you today in what you read.* Be prepared to write down what you hear, feel or sense the Lord is speaking to your heart.

*See appendix 1 regarding *logos* and *rhema* words from God.

Encouragement in Action

Costco Gas

Several years ago God gave me the perfect opportunity to hear His voice. I stood at the Costco gas pump preparing to fill my vehicle when suddenly an image flashed through my mind of gas overflowing out of the nozzle. My first thought was, *Okay, the Lord is warning me so I don't get covered in gas.* I was lost in the image when I heard gas pouring all over the pavement, followed by a loud string of swear words. I leaned around my side of the island to see a woman frantically trying to control the nozzle with gas spraying everywhere.

I have shared this story with others, and the first question they ask me is, "Why would God show you that?" The experience had long passed and my answer was always the same: I figured I had simply missed the rest of the story. A friend challenged me to take a minute and ask God the same question. I prayed and quickly heard the word *aware.* To confirm my impression, I asked my friend, "What is God showing you?" She prayed briefly and said, "I see you talking to God, and your response is, 'I hear You.'" God showed me that I could hear Him speak. He wanted me to be aware of His voice in order for me to take the next step. In the moment I could have asked God, "Why are You showing me this? Is there something I need to do or someone I need to warn?" Now I know.

> The sheep listen to his voice. He calls his own sheep by name and leads them out. When he has brought out all his own, he goes on ahead of them, and his sheep follow him *because they know his voice. But they will never follow a stranger; in fact, they will run away from him because they do not recognize a stranger's voice.*
>
> John 10:3–5, emphasis added

Do you recall when God may have shown you something, but you had no idea what to do with it or just shrugged it off as the strangest thing? Shannon was a freshman in high school and preparing to move to a different city when she had the following dream:

In my dream I was standing in a crowd that had gathered in front of a house. In the center of the crowd was a tall, slender-looking kid whom I had never met, but he appeared to be directing us to play our instruments. Behind him was an elderly man with his wife, both dressed in pajamas and looking quite amused. Suddenly an angry man came charging up the lawn of the house, grabbed the slender kid by his shirt and slammed him up against a car. He screamed profanities and was extremely irate that we were playing music in the middle of the night. I thought to myself, *Well, if he knows this happens every year, why doesn't he just get a condo elsewhere?* Then I woke up.

Shannon went on to share that within a year her family relocated to a new state. She joined her high school's marching band and spent every afternoon memorizing music and field marching maneuvers. One evening, as per tradition, the band marched to the band director's house and played their musical ensemble at midnight. Suddenly the dream she had received from God months prior began to unfold. An eerie sense of *déjà vu* drifted upon her.

Before Shannon could say anything or warn anybody, the man she saw charging up the lawn in her dream did just that and slammed the drum major against the car. The same inner thought she had in her dream sprang to mind, and the weight of reality settled on her. For the longest time she thought, *I could have warned our drum major. I should have known to do something.*

After that night, the tradition of the midnight marches held fast, but only with a police escort.

Activation Prayer

Lord Jesus, I come before You today and ask You to open my eyes and ears to hear and see from You. Help me to be aware when You are speaking and help me not to miss it. Lord, show me times in the past that I may have missed You speaking. Teach me and show me what I need to learn so that I can do better next time. I thank You that Your Word promises I can and will hear Your voice and I won't follow the voice of a stranger.

Go Deeper

- Are you aware of God's voice speaking to you?

- Have you had a time when God might have shown you something, but you had no idea what to do with it or simply shrugged it off as the strangest thing? Write it out. Then reflect on what you could have done differently and what your next steps should have been.

• Read Job 33:15–18. What does this passage in the book of Job say about the specific way God can speak?

8

Open Doors

While on church staff as an administrator I was asked to join a mission team in hosting a conference in Romania. The worship pastor I worked for was to lead the music, and the senior pastor's wife, Jane, was the conference speaker. My job seemed simple; I would assist both as their "backstage girl." But God had bigger plans for my trip to Romania than I ever thought possible! Don't you love how His plans are better than ours?

On our drive to the airport one team member excitedly asked, "Oh! Debbie, how are the classes going? I hear you're doing some awesome prophetic ministry." She kept peppering me with questions and pushing me for details until Pastor Jane held up her finger.

"Wait a minute," she said. "You're teaching prophetic classes? Tell me more." I told her what I was learning and shared about stepping out in my newly discovered teaching gift. Pastor Jane listened patiently and then said, "If God ever gives you a word for me I would love to hear it." I smiled politely and immediately mentally pushed aside her request because I felt unqualified.

Upon our arrival in Romania we were put on a bus to travel to our hotel. Because many of us had never been to eastern Europe, the tour guide shared the history of Romania and explained the places we were seeing. As I stared out at the snow-covered streets the Lord began speaking to me. I was exhausted from the travel, and rather than welcome His voice I was filled with anxiety. Was this God? Was this really a word for Jane, or was I only creating the voice because Jane had talked to me in the car? I quickly imagined the humiliation of delivering the word and her apologetic smile. "Poor Debbie. She's not really prophetic, but she tries. She's so sweet."

After settling in our rooms I asked my boss, Pastor Laurie, to share the word with Jane so I could avoid the embarrassment. The next morning when I woke up and went into the kitchen Jane was waiting for me. Laurie had obviously spoken to her. As I made my toast, she inquired, "So, I hear the Lord gave you a word for me."

I stammered, "What? Huh? Well, no. I wouldn't exactly call it a word."

She pulled me aside and proceeded to position me in the light coming through the little Romanian kitchen window so she could see me more fully and said, "When you speak prophetically, there's this passionate fire that comes over you; I can see it in your eyes." She finished positioning me and said, "Good. Now go ahead."

I gave her the word, and even though I cannot remember it exactly I remember her reaction. She was touched by it. She had been wrestling with God, asking if the message she had prepared could possibly be for the Romanian women. She informed God there was no way she could share this word without confirmation. She explained that when we were all on the bus and the guide talked about the culture of Romania, one of the themes that stood out was the wild dog problem. They were roaming the streets, and we were warned to steer clear of them. Pastor Jane shared that the Lord wanted her to speak on the passage of Scripture about the lady coming to Jesus and telling Him that even the dogs get to eat the scraps from His table (see Matthew 15:27). The word

I shared with her confirmed what God had already spoken. She could now preach her message with confidence. Brick by brick, my walls of self-doubt and insecurity were coming down. When I returned from my mission trip to Romania, something shifted. God began a new work in me. At the time, I did not know what was taking place, but I knew God was opening new doors.

He gave me a dream.

June 3, 2004

I was in a car traveling down a wide-open, straight stretch of highway with the administrative/finance pastor from church beside me in the passenger seat. The sky was gold and radiating light.

When I awoke I remember thinking to myself during the dream that it felt familiar, as if I had been given this dream before. I took some time to go through my past dream journals to see what else I could find. In looking, I found not one dream but two, with different dates yet the same topic. The dream below was particularly exciting because I had received it several months earlier.

January 24, 2004

The dream started out with me speaking, teaching, maybe even preaching. Then I was sitting at a table with mail sitting in front of me. I began to go through the mail and opened the envelopes with an old-fashioned letter opener. As I opened them, cash and checks began falling out on the desk in front of me, and then I woke up.

At the time of this dream I was still working at the church. Our prophetic speaker from several months earlier came into my office, and I took the opportunity to ask her about it.

She said, "Oh, that's simple. The Lord is going to provide for you. It is like a ministry—something similar to my ministry— and money won't be a problem because money will be coming in the mail. People will partner with you because of what God has called you to do."

God is faithful! I realize now that my dreams not only helped to confirm my direction, but they also held a deeper and more specific meaning. The dreams were revealing God's promise and provision for my own ministry yet to be born. If I had not written them down I would not have remembered. I was able to go back and confirm God's plan for me. The finances were going to be okay; but more than that, He was beginning to open doors into new territory for me.

Just as God was faithful to me, He is faithful to others. He longs to open doors for us to minister in our gifting. I have a friend who shared with me that the Lord has been very consistent to open ministry doors. When she was in Bible college she was able to discern several of her gifts. When God wants her to step out in a particular gifting she said an opportunity appears in front of her. I asked her to describe exactly what she was talking about, and she said, "I will either overhear a conversation or someone describing exactly what I know I can contribute; or the Lord will show me a picture, and I can see exactly where He needs me to serve."

One time she visited a church and could see they needed small groups and a program for new visitors. She then wrote up a step-by-step plan. That plan turned into her job description, because they hired her! For my friend, the Lord opens doors and gives her favor with the people she is to serve.

I know others who have similar testimonies. They start out thinking God has one thing for them to do and then realize through life circumstances that there is a bigger picture they never saw.

Melodi always had a heart for the nations. She had traveled overseas many times and thought she would always be involved in overseas church ministry. After an eight-year season serving as an associate pastor and just months before she gave birth to her son, she resigned from her position, but it was her intention to return to ministry once her child was a little older. When her son was diagnosed with type 1 diabetes (T1D), an autoimmune disease, however, she found herself in an entirely new ministry field.

Melodi and her family have lived with this disease for over three years, and she is now creating a nonprofit organization that will come alongside T1D children and their families to provide resources, support and education. She is also developing a vision to send equipment and supplies overseas where T1D assistance is not available for children who need it. Melodi said, "I am still shepherding people, and I am still going to be involved overseas!"

I know God longs for you to experience His plans and His dreams for your life. Just as God opens doors into new territory for my friends and me, allow Him to guide and direct you as He opens doors for you.

Go Deeper

- Do you struggle with fear or anxiety getting in the way as you step out in ministry? Write about it. Ask the Holy Spirit to reveal to you what specific fears are holding you back from stepping out and what might be the root of those fears. Then ask Him to set you free from those fears so that you can charge ahead.

- What does Romans 8:14–16 say about fear?

- Have you ever thought you were to do one thing, only to discover God had other or even bigger plans?

Activation Prayer

Jesus, thank You that I am no longer a slave to fear and anxiety. God, break the bondages of things in my life that are holding me back from fully serving You. Speak to me about the plans You have for my life. God, show me where my thinking is too small, and infuse me with Your plans. God, begin to direct me toward the open doors You have for me.

Activate Encouragement

Choose someone you know with a specific prayer need. Take a minute and ask God to speak to you specifically about what He would have you pray for the person and situation. Jot down key thoughts, phrases or Scripture references that come to mind. Once you have done this, write a prayer using the things God spoke to you. Once you have written out the prayer, contact the individual and share what God had you pray.

9

Put It on the Altar:
Testing Prophecy

Dear friends, do not believe every spirit, but test the spirits to
see whether they are from God, because many false prophets
have gone out into the world.

1 John 4:1

As noted in 1 John, we are to test prophecies and everything of a
spiritual nature. If it does not hold up against the Word of God,
which is *truth*, then we are to get rid of it. Many of us have been
spiritually wounded because we did not test prophetic words
spoken to us in Jesus' name. The Scriptures warn us, "Watch
out for false prophets. They come to you in sheep's clothing,
but inwardly they are ferocious wolves" (Matthew 7:15).

Everyone, regardless of his or her gifting, has a responsibility to
test what is spoken and ask God to confirm its validity. We must
also hold it up to Scripture and search His Word for truth. The
prophetic word and the Word of God must line up. A true word
from God will never contradict Scripture or His nature. If we do
not test before we act, we open ourselves to considerable heartache.

We are responsible to seek direction from God first, not people. Hunting for answers in the wrong places took me on a life detour for almost two years. I waffled back and forth, whining, "Is this what God has for me?" until I tired of hearing my own voice. I cannot imagine how God must have felt. Even when He did try to speak to me, I could not hear Him over my own doubt.

How Do We Test or Judge Prophecy?

> Therefore encourage one another and build each other up, just as in fact you are doing. . . . Rejoice always, pray continually, give thanks in all circumstances; for this is God's will for you in Christ Jesus. Do not quench the Spirit. Do not treat prophecies with contempt but test them all; hold on to what is good, reject every kind of evil.
>
> 1 Thessalonians 5:11, 16–22

This Scripture tells us that not only do we need to encourage and build each other up, but we must also test everything and hold on to what is good. It is the responsibility of those receiving a prophetic word to judge the word and pray over what is spoken to them. Do not act without confirmation from God. Even if a word is spoken corporately, you should apply the same guidelines.

Before applying the following questions, take a moment and pray, asking God to show you and help you discern what is of Him and what is not. Here are some questions to consider as you test or judge prophetic words.

1. Does the word spoken line up with Scripture?

   a. If yes, proceed to the next question.

   b. If no, then stop. There is no need to proceed further, because God will never contradict Himself.

2. Does the word spoken resonate in your spirit?

First John 2:20 instructs us, "But you have an anointing from the Holy One, and all of you know the truth." Because the Holy Spirit dwells within us, we all have discernment within our spirit that tells us when something is wrong. Discernment is not a feeling! It is communication with the Holy Spirit. Prophecies should ring true within our spirit. This can be challenging. We are human, so by our sin nature, we fail. The quality of our discernment is directly related to our relationship with God. The deeper and more mature our relationship, the more accurate our ability to discern.

3. Does the word spoken confirm something specifically to you?

If a word does not confirm a current situation or issue, it does not necessarily mean the person speaking the word is wrong. It could mean that it is not pertaining to a current issue but a future one.

If this is the case, put the word on the shelf and ask God to remind you if/when the time is right. There are times when a prophecy is not quite ready for prime time. I have delivered words for the future, and in those moments it is difficult to know if I missed it.

One time I was asked to do prophetic ministry at a women's event, and I was ministering to a woman who had never experienced prophetic encouragement. She was extremely hesitant even about receiving ministry, but she respected some of the other women who were there and decided I must be okay.

When I prayed for Debra I got a word about her current job situation that was right on, but then I saw the letter *A* and felt it was a person who was very significant in her life. She shook her head and said nope; she did not know anyone with a name that began with *A*. We both thought I had misheard God, and we forgot all about it.

Fast forward to eight years later. Debra shared with me how in a recent move she had found the recorded ministry session. She was blown away. Debra now has a five-year-old granddaughter whom she cares for on a regular basis, and you guessed it—her name begins with the letter *A*. Not only that, but little Adeline's mother was told by doctors she would never have children because she previously battled cancer. God is good, and He is faithful to fulfill His promises. When Debra needed assurance of God's faithfulness, He did so by reminding her of the message spoken years prior.

Now What?

Once you have determined the word is from God, how should you proceed? This is where the rubber meets the road. I have given countless words that were never received or implemented in spite of their accuracy. I have watched word after word fall to the floor, never to be picked up. I know the importance of a prophetic word from the Lord. Given at the right time, it has the power to set people free.

As I ministered to a young couple one Sunday I kept seeing a light bulb over the man's head flashing on and off repeatedly. I knew it had something to do with inventions. When I shared the picture I asked the man point-blank, "You have these light-bulb moments, don't you? You get ideas and thoughts. Are you an inventor?"

He just stared blankly. No response.

I questioned him further. "Do you get information and ideas, but you don't know what to do with them?"

Still no response. It was so silent you could have heard a cricket chirping softly somewhere nearby. I know sometimes people do not want to give any information for fear I might "cheat" spiritually. However, when no response is given, it makes it difficult for me to know if I am discerning correctly what I am hearing, not to mention if he or she is willing to receive.

As they continued to stare at me, I was a bit less patient. "I actually need a little acknowledgment from you. Are you indeed an inventor?"

He reluctantly responded, "Well, yeah."

It was not much to go on, but I continued to share what God showed me. God gifted him with the brilliant mind of an inventor, and He would continue to download blueprints and ideas for inventions he was supposed to develop. When I finished, the husband looked at his wife and said, "This is really interesting because we just talked to a patent lawyer last week."

My head bobbed in surprise. "You talked to a patent lawyer about an invention?"

"Yes."

I took a deep breath, trying to find my patience. "Well, it looks to me like God is speaking directly to you about a current situation and confirming the plans He has for you."

They shook their heads back and forth in disagreement slowly. "Well, you know, we're not really certain what God wants, and we are not even sure if we are to pursue this whole invention patent thing."

On the inside I was silently screaming, *You have got to be kidding me, right? How much clearer do you want it? God just downloaded His heart!* Instead, I smiled and bit my tongue. Part of their unbelief was their inexperience with prophecy, and it was not my place to convince them.

It is important to leave room for people to come to God for themselves. They would have to make a choice to accept and believe the word—or not. *Oh, Lord,* I inwardly prayed, *please don't let this be a word that falls to the floor.*

One final consideration when testing a prophetic word is to evaluate the source. The following verse cautions us to be discerning about whom we listen to. No one is perfect and without issue, which is why we are advised to look at the spiritual fruit in people's lives to determine their maturity and character.

> *By their fruit you will recognize them.* Do people pick grapes from thorn bushes, or figs from thistles? Likewise, every good tree bears good fruit, but a bad tree bears bad fruit. A good tree cannot bear bad fruit, and a bad tree cannot bear good fruit.
>
> Matthew 7:16–18, emphasis added

Bob serves on staff at a church in Texas and is someone whom I mentor in the prophetic gift of encouragement. One night as Bob was on the way to a softball game he asked the Lord to lead him to someone who needed an encouraging word. The name *Franklin* came to mind. Here is what Bob shared about this experience:

> As I got the name *Franklin*, I also got a word. This word came with a heavy weightiness that settled on me so strongly I sensed a grave situation and began to intercede:
>
> *I see you.*
> *I know what you are going through.*
> *Breathe.*
> *I've got it all under control.*
> *My eye is on you. You are never out of My sight.*
> *Take heart!*
>
> I wasn't at the field long before the Lord led me to a man named Franklin. We engaged in small talk while I mustered the courage to ask how he was doing. "Fine," was his response, so I pressed a bit further, letting him know I'd been praying for him and wondered how he was really doing. I still received a drawn-out, "Fine," with a look of dismissal. This was early on in my learning how to hear from God for others, and I was super afraid to give a wrong word. As a result I often checked

for some type of confirmation beforehand. Hence my "How are you really?" question.

A bit embarrassed that I must have totally missed it, I turned to walk away, when for some unknown reason I looked back and asked, "Is anything coming?" His face blanched. His eyes widened then darkened and drooped as he responded, "Yes."

I said, "Okay, that's all I needed to know. Then this is for you," and I gave him the word, including the pacing, sense of weightiness and the tangible feeling of God's total care and concern for him.

A couple months later I found out that at the time of our conversation he had been preparing for a devastating and inevitable situation that would negatively affect his life for years to come.

God sure knows what He's doing, and my faith and trust continue to grow as I partner with Him.

Go Deeper

- Read 1 Thessalonians 5:11–22. What stands out to you most in these verses regarding prophetic encouragement?

- Why do you think God tells us to test words that are spoken?

Activation Prayer

Father, I want to be an encourager, just as 1 Thessalonians 5:11 instructs. Help me be someone who builds others up with my words. May my words be filled with joy and life. Help me know when to speak and when not to speak. Help me to know what is You and what is not You. Allow Your Spirit of discernment to be evident in my life, and show me Your heart concerning things.

Activate Encouragement

Find one or more Scriptures to back up a prophetic word of encouragement you have given or someone has given to you.

For example, as you read the encouraging word Bob spoke to Franklin, what Scripture comes to mind that backs up what was spoken? One example might be Matthew 6:25–26, in which God cares for the birds of the air.

10

Hear God First

What was I created to do? On some level, each of us searches for answers to this essential and life-changing question. I have perpetually asked two questions: What plans does God have for me? And, am I in God's will?

More than a year after I traveled to Romania, doors were indeed opening. When I was asked to speak and travel with Anne, a gifted speaker and recognized prophet, I began to wonder if this was the calling God had for me as well. She quickly became my mentor.

On the second morning of a retreat in Montana, as Anne and I got ready for the day, I blurted out, "Can I ask you a question? Do you think God has called me to be a prophet?"

Her quick response caught me off guard. "No, not at all. It's not what He has for you."

I was taken aback, but by now I had grown bold enough to question her. "Why not?" I asked.

She explained I indeed have the gift. I was a good speaker and could prophesy, but I was not called to be a prophet. She went on to explain what it took to be a prophet—that I would walk a long, dark, lonely road and experience some seasons of feeling isolated and alone.

I felt discouraged and needed to escape the room for a while, so I went down the hall to the hotel's breakfast room. As I sat there eating I struggled internally. Her words did not sit well with me. I was not searching for the title of prophet; I just wanted to know my purpose.

As I rehashed the conversation, the Lord said to me, *What about Elisha and Elijah?* It came out of the blue. I knew the story but not enough to know what God might be trying to tell me. I began reading the Scriptures regarding Elijah fleeing to the mountain and complaining to God (see 1 Kings 18–19).

Elijah was running away from Jezebel, who threatened to kill him. Elijah's complaint to God was that he was the only prophet left and God should feel sorry for him. God then sent Elijah back down the mountain in the direction he had come to find a young man named Elisha. When Elijah found him, he was directed by God to throw his mantle over Elisha. In doing so, there was an immediate, supernatural change in Elisha. I was reminded of the first time I met Anne and witnessed the ministry of the prophetic. At the time, something changed in me.

As I continued to read I discovered Elisha left everything to follow Elijah and become his apprentice. During this time he watched and learned. It was essentially a prophetic apprenticeship. The Bible says Elijah tried to get Elisha to leave him alone, but he wouldn't. At one point he asked Elisha, "What is it that you want?"

Elisha responded, "I want a double portion of the anointing and mantle that's on your life."

Elijah said, "If you see me taken to heaven—if you're there and you see me being taken—then it shall be as you have asked." As Elijah was taken to heaven in a whirlwind, his mantle dropped, and Elisha picked it up. Scripture confirms Elisha indeed received a double portion of Elijah's ministry!

As I sat reading I thought, *Okay, but what exactly does this mean?* God was showing me that Elisha did not go through a challenging season of isolation and hardship; Elisha was trained on the job.

After I finished reading I went back to our room, where Anne was continuing to get ready. I sat on the edge of my bed watching her iron. It took me a moment to work up my courage and share what God showed me during breakfast. When I finally spoke I explained how the Lord reminded me of the story of Elijah and Elisha. "Isn't our relationship like theirs?" I asked.

Her response was immediate. "No. Why are you bringing this up?"

I swallowed hard. "Well, you said I am not called to be a prophet or walk in the gifting of one because I haven't been through the challenging seasons they face, but Elisha didn't either. He was called by God, and a mantle of prophecy was placed over his shoulders by Elijah."

She held her ground, and I could tell that was the end of the conversation. I was hurt by the strength of her words and how adamant she was that this was not what God had for me. She was my mentor, and I trusted she spoke on behalf of the Lord.

At this retreat we shared speaking duties, but my responsibilities included running the product table and answering any questions that might arise. As the morning session was wrapping up, an older woman approached me and asked for prayer. As I bowed my head and began, she interrupted me, looked me in the eyes and said, "You and Anne are just like Elijah and Elisha." I smiled to myself. God certainly has a sense of humor. I responded, "Wow, that's really interesting. You should tell Anne." God was confirming I had heard Him correctly.

In the several years I spent ministering with Anne, I matured. I learned valuable lessons about the importance of trusting my ability to hear the Holy Spirit and live out His calling on my life. This experience specifically taught me about how to test and discern if counsel and prophetic words spoken over me are on target and what to do when they are not. Today, I am a pastor who is speaking, teaching and ministering in the prophetic, and for that I am grateful.

I have been asked many times why it is so much easier to listen to others than hear God for ourselves. I am clear on this: God wants to speak to you about you. Spend time with Him so you can hear what He is saying about your future and His plans for you.

Jeremiah 29:11 says, "'For I know the plans I have for you,' declares the LORD." God is the One who wants to breathe into your spirit and impart to you His plans and purposes for your life. He does not want you to get your marching orders from anyone else. All too often people make the mistake of basing their decisions on what others think, not on what God is telling them. Get your direction from God!

Both Su and Linda had similar experiences of looking to others instead of God for direction and confirmation. Su thought she had to have someone's approval for what God was telling her, especially from leadership in the church. Years ago Su was in a church that believed the pastor and elders were right under God. She said, "They had to approve everything you did in life. If they said no or that you weren't ready, you had to stop following that path or be kicked out of church." For many years Su shut down her prophetic gift because it got her in trouble with leadership.

Linda believed God was guiding her to step out in the community to pray for people who shared a need or request. She was getting very positive responses and was excited to share testimonies during Wednesday-night church of how God was using her. It seemed she had something to share each week. After a while she began to feel self-conscious, so she stopped sharing. Even though people were receptive to receive prayer in public, her family was embarrassed. Linda eventually stopped altogether. Looking back, she believes she started listening to the enemy and was influenced by people's opinions and drew back. Every person has a responsibility to confirm what God is speaking to him or her. Even if someone is deemed prophetically gifted or a prophet, his or her words should be tested. If I could go back in time I would follow my own advice (and I know Su and Linda would too). Instead of taking my questions to anyone else I would first take them to the Lord.

Go Deeper

- Do you know what God has created you to do? If so, what is it? If not, what do you think is holding you back from knowing?

- Why do you think it is easier to listen to others than to hear God for ourselves?

Activation Prayer

Father God, release Your Spirit and breathe into my life. Blow through the dry and broken places and impart Your plans and purposes to me. God, release Your will for my life. Show me what You would have me do for You. If I am doing something that is not what You have called me to do, please show me. God, I look to You and You alone, not to others, for direction. Guide me, teach me, show me the way to walk, and I will.

Activate Encouragement

Jeremiah 29:11 tells us that God has plans for us. We just prayed a prayer asking God to show us His will for our life, so take the time to listen and allow His Spirit to move upon your heart and speak to you today. Ask Him specifically what His plans are for your life, then write or journal what you feel He is saying. Pray over and into it, proactively pressing into the words He has given you, proclaiming them and taking action when needed. God will be faithful to confirm and validate what He has spoken to you.

Think on It!

We like to label things with titles. It helps us define roles and de-termine importance, responsibility and authority. For me, titles are something I run from, especially the title of prophet. The im-portance is not whether I am a prophet or not but whether I am being obedient to God's calling on my life. From God's point of view there is nothing exclusive or elite about being an apostle, a prophet, a pastor, a teacher or an evangelist.

Having these callings does not make you or me a super Christian. These are job descriptions or functions within the governmental structure of the Church. A person who is called to operate in one of these offices is called to do a job. Simply put, it is God who provides gifts and callings; they are not shiny rewards to earn.

I am not called to be an evangelist, but this should not stop me from evangelizing or sharing the Gospel. I think the same could be said of any one of the offices. If you are called to an office, then be obedient to God's prompting and serve. Likewise, if you are not called to an office, then it is vital you not fake it.

> Not many of you should become teachers, my fellow believers, be-cause you know that we who teach will be judged more strictly.
>
> James 3:1

I like to ask people the following questions:

- Do you need a title to do what God has called you to do?
- Have you ever found yourself seeking a title or position?
- Do you need to introduce yourself to others using a title?

The answer should be no. If it is not, it may indicate a wrong heart attitude. Jesus did not go around telling people He was God's Son, the Savior of the world. Instead, He let His life and ministry to others speak for itself. I, too, would rather my gifting speak for itself. I would rather be judged by the fruit of my ministry (see Matthew 7:17) than by a name tag on my shirt. If I concern myself with claiming the title of prophet I risk hindering the people God has asked me to serve.

A pastor shared the following story regarding the importance of understanding why we do not need a titled position to serve God:

> During a prayer group at church we prayed intensely for a famous pastor of a worldwide ministry, and then we prayed briefly for a woman in our church who sewed teddy bears for kids in hospitals. The Lord interrupted the lead pastor and told us that God considered the ministries equally important to His Kingdom, and we should pray with the same intensity for the woman in our church.

Our identity is found in Christ and serving Him, not in positions or titles.

Activation Prayer

Jesus, help me keep my eyes focused on You as I step out to obey the calling You have placed in my life. Help me not seek recognition or titles from anyone. I choose to walk in the gifts You have given me. Lord, may my life produce good fruit and be pleasing to You.

Go Deeper

- Read Matthew 7:15–20 and John 15:1–8. What do these passages say about good fruit versus bad fruit?

- What good fruit can others see in your life and ministry?

11

Danger Zones

In life, there are positives and negatives in all we say and do. The good always outweighs the bad, and we should never allow the negative to stop us from pursuing the good. As we move forward in the gift of encouragement we should keep our eyes focused on the positive. It is good, however, to be mindful of the negative so we can move forward with purpose. Below is a brief list of danger zones I have encountered within the prophetic.

- Negativity
- Pride
- Control
- Self-righteousness
- Entitlement
- Arrogance
- Depression
- Disobedience
- Delayed obedience (taking a long time to respond to a word from the Lord)

- Not taking time to hear/taking too much time to hear
- Judgmentalism
- Taking self too seriously
- Seeking gifts rather than the Giver of the gifts
- Projection/personal agenda
- Lacking love
- Over-spiritualizing
- Taking on the responsibility of making it come to pass
- Over-explaining what you hear
- Downplaying what you hear

I am sure there are more pitfalls than those listed above, but these are the most common issues I have encountered.

Negativity

Sometimes when the Lord speaks to us the message can seem harsh or negative. Before you share these tough-nut messages, pray about them! Often there is a deeper, almost hidden encouraging word just below the hard exterior. Remember, the spiritual gift of prophecy should be encouraging and building up, not beating up.

A woman once asked to pray for me because she was blessed by the ministry she received. As she prayed for me, she shared that God revealed my children would be in a car accident, but she prayed against it and that no harm would come to them. She truly believed she was speaking out encouragement and operating in the gift of prophecy. I knew she was not. She was not speaking words of encouragement at all. In fact, her words could have left me fearful and anxious every time my children drove or were in a car.

Trust me when I say it is important for people to discern God's voice. This type of prophecy on the fly can be both good and bad. We all hear God differently, and when people are equipped to tune out any voice of negativity and listen only to the voice of truth, lives are blessed. When people are filled with the hope and promise of what God has shared it is life changing. When we encourage one another it is powerful! A ministry friend shared this story about a time when she received a negative word. While listening to the Father's heart for the person, she was able to extend His love into the situation.

I was on the altar ministry team for people who came forward for prayer. Although I knew God spoke to me, I was less sure how to bring a word or even if it was okay to share when it was really personal. On one occasion I approached a woman kneeling at the front when, in the spirit, I very plainly heard, *She is in sin.* Immediately I began to struggle in my mind. I said to the Lord, *I sin! I'm not going to tell her that [judge her, accuse her, be holier than thou, etc.]!* There was only silence. *Okay, but how do I say it?* I asked. *Tell her I love her, and there is nothing she can do that can't be forgiven and washed by My sacrifice on the cross.* As I shared this message with her, her head popped up, she burst into tears and she fell into my arms. Shocked, I repeated it and assured her how much Jesus loved her.

A few weeks later the oversight pastor called me into his office, which was not the usual policy, and asked me what had happened. I shared, and he said that explained her breakthrough. She had been in an extramarital affair. Her husband knew and wanted to stay and work through it, but she was reluctant. After prayer she repented and decided to end the affair and enter into counseling with her husband. I was so grateful the Lord was teaching me early to be careful how things are said. He wants people healed and set free, not condemned!

The Danger of Pride

There is serious danger with pride. It is bad. It is not complicated. I am not talking about the kind of pride you take in your work. I am talking about the type of pride God condemns in the Bible. We have all been around people who are so full of themselves there is no room for anyone else to stand. Scripture is clear: Pride is a sin, and we must guard ourselves from it.

Several years ago at one of our prophetic leadership meetings we invited several people from other congregations to our class. It was not uncommon for pastors to ask Anne to provide prophetic training, and often others would join us for practice sessions. Most of the time they would fit right in and become regular members. One of these sessions stands out in my memory.

A pastor warned Anne before the practice session, "Jim is a prophetic individual who is accurate and hears God, but we do not know how to handle him." When he arrived to meet our group, it was immediately clear what the issue was. He was full of himself, and he was clearly not submitted to anyone. He tried to insert himself in the leadership and came surprisingly close to taking over the meeting. As soon as he left, the rest of us wondered, *What just happened? Who is this guy?* Jim was an atmosphere-changer and not in a good way. He was accurate, but Jim embodied the resounding gong Scripture talks about (see 1 Corinthians 13:1). There was so much pride surrounding him that no one wanted any part of it.

Attitude of Entitlement

There are a lot of prophetic people who are relentlessly looking for a position and a platform to be heard. No one should fight for position. Only God places people in positions of leadership and authority. The only entitlement any of us should have is that of a servant. Jesus told us that if we want to become great in the Kingdom we need to be like children (see Matthew 18:2–4; 23:12). We are told in Luke 10:27 to "love your neighbor as yourself," and Luke 14:11 tells us that "those who humble themselves will be exalted." Take time to read Psalm 37:11, 29 about meekness and righteousness.

The Arrogant "I'm Right" Mentality

This mentality says, "I'm right," and leaves no room for any other perspective, discussion, debate or judgment. While there may be times you are right, there are also times when you are wrong. This goes back to issues of the heart and having pure intentions.

Friends of mine experienced this mentality upon revisiting a church. They liked the church so much that they were considering making it their home church. At the end of the service the husband decided to go forward for prayer over his chronic foot pain.

While he waited for an available team a woman asked why he had come forward. He explained his desire to be healed. He wanted prayer for the chronic foot pain and the numbness and explained how the doctors had not been much help. The woman immediately began prophesying over him, and the words she said were something to this effect: "You are an evangelist, and the reason you are having problems with your feet is because you aren't utilizing your gift. When you start sharing your faith openly with other people your healing will come." She also mentioned the Bible verse that talks about "how beautiful are the feet of those who bring good news" (see Isaiah 52:7). That was it.

He walked away with a very uncomfortable feeling, knowing that prophetic words are meant to be encouraging in nature, not straight-out admonishment, and he knew in his spirit that this word was totally false. I asked him how it made him feel, and this is what he shared with me:

> This woman didn't know me. She had no idea I am the type of person who pretty much shares my faith with everyone, even before knowing their stance on things. My sharing is, in fact, so open that it has gotten me in trouble from time to time! I don't

claim to have the spiritual gift of evangelism, but certainly I am not afraid to share the Gospel. Since this woman was a pastor on staff and head over their prayer and prophetic ministry team it was disconcerting that she was so far off in what she spoke over me. This was ultimately one of the determining factors in our decision not to make this our home church.

Sadly, he never received prayer for healing. This ministry leader had a mentality of arrogance, thinking she knew what he needed, and ignored his prayer request.

Projection/Personal Agenda

The danger zone of projection or personal agenda is a sticky one. At its core, it is simply when someone projects his or her will or opinion onto a person in the form of a prophetic word. It can seem harmless enough, especially if the person is right; yet this is where so much hurt in the body of Christ comes from.

Well-meaning people can project what they think is best onto someone else either innocently or purposefully. I know because I have been guilty of doing this with my children. Just ask them. I used to have control issues so bad that my poor children did not have any fun.

When I first began to step out in the prophetic the Lord began to deal with my control issues. He began dealing with my instinct to project and harbor a personal agenda, as well as almost every danger zone characteristic. In truth, I could share a personal story for each of these areas where God had to walk me through and show me how to handle them appropriately so I would not hurt anyone.

I tell many stories on myself now, but back then it was not so funny. At the base of control is fear. Fear comes in many forms and affects people differently. Control is usually a person's way of creating a safe place around them when they are fearful about something. For me, it was fear of what people would think. What would they think if my Christmas tree was not decorated perfectly with all the lights spaced evenly apart or if all the ornaments were not placed correctly or the ribbon tied perfectly? You know the old adage "Mother knows best"? Well, trust me; this mom was armed with a *knowing*. I knew how to project what I felt my children should and should not be doing with their lives. Now, this may shock you, but I was one of those moms who would tell my children what they were doing wrong and why it was wrong in God's eyes. Over time I learned that when I used the information as ammunition to call my children out, not only did it hurt my relationship with them, but it also hindered their relationship with the Lord. It gave them no room to work through their stuff, it left no space for them to come to their own repentance, and it definitely did not leave room for the Holy Spirit to convict them. I was doing it all myself.

Today I have a great relationship with my kids, but only because I have apologized, repented and told them that I would not wield my prophetic gift as a weapon. They know they have the choice to come to me if they want to know what God has to say about a situation or a person. I have learned to ask permission before dumping knowledge on them.

I know we do not want to think that someone would force personal agendas onto someone else, but it can and does happen, especially when it comes to prophetic encouragement. Have you ever just *known* that a certain someone should not be in a relationship with someone else? Yes? Me too. Here is the thing: We may be right on and even discerning the information to be correct, but we must pray for that person's eyes to be opened instead of heading straight into their space and confronting them regarding their terrible choice. It is not loving or kind and could be received differently if handled better.

Remember, when God corrects or confronts us, He does so out of love. He comes alongside and speaks truth to us, all the while drawing us into a deeper relationship with Himself. When we confront someone with what we perceive, we must make sure that it is not just our natural senses or eyes picking it up but that it is from the Lord. We need to give people space and grace to process what we share and allow the Lord to speak to them regarding it as well.

When I do this, I often find two things. First, the Holy Spirit will have already been speaking to the individual, so that when I am given a word that contains sensitive information about that person, it will be confirmation of what God had already been showing him or her. Second, the Holy Spirit will share sensitive information with individuals who are already in close relationship with one another, who have an established basis of trust, who have a pure heart and who do not have ulterior motives.

Lacking Love

Many prophetic people I know have insensitive or abrasive personalities. Being a direct person is not bad; however, when your words and actions lack love, people turn away. If you are used to speaking your mind, that is fine. Do it how Jesus did: in love. Jesus did not mince words or worry about hurting people's feelings with the truth because He took every step in love. It is all in the delivery. Also, it is important that you not add your own advice or say words such as, "I say this out of love," before sharing something unkind. It does not soften the blow and only reinforces your apathy.

Go Deeper

- Read 1 Corinthians 13.

- Why is love so important when operating in spiritual gifts?

- Have you ever met someone who was truly gifted but did not walk in love? What did you think of his or her ministry?

- Read Proverbs 4:23. Why is it so important to guard our heart?

Activation Prayer

God, I pray as King David prayed: Search me, know my heart and test me. If I have anything offensive or anxious in me, please reveal it and heal it. God, help me always to be motivated by love and not be a resounding gong. Lord, I want to help people, not hurt them. Show me if I have fallen into any of these danger zone areas. Forgive me and renew and purify my heart before You.

Activate Encouragement

Ask God to share an encouraging word with you for a specific individual. It may be the person at the drive-thru window, the clerk at the store, a person in line with you or your waiter. If you can, write it down. If not, then share verbally with the person what God has given you.

12

Help Wanted: ~~Perfect~~ Ordinary People Only

When it comes to the prophetic, there are some serious extremes. On one side, there are the folks who love it and cannot get enough of it. They tend to be thought of as unhealthy fanatics. Church leaders try diligently to keep a good distance between these fanatics and the flock. On the opposite end of the spectrum are those who are staunchly opposed to any hint of the prophetic. They question why we do not continue the Old Testament practice of stoning a failed prophet (see Deuteronomy 13:5; 18:20–22), and they reject the freelance nature of the Holy Spirit speaking through anyone. As far as they are concerned, prophecy died with Jesus and is not for today.

Those who run fast and far from the perceived threat of the prophetic are missing out on a beneficial gift that can truly edify others. Prophecy today is not about the prophet; rather, it is about the restoration of communication between the Father and His children through the Holy Spirit. God is personal and alive. He has extended His grace and no longer seeks to stone those who get it wrong. He simply wants us to offer others daily hope, encouragement and comfort.

God calls us all to operate in the spiritual gift of prophecy, but the problem is that some think if they can hear from God they are, in fact, a prophet. Some take on this image and begin to speak on behalf of God when in reality they are speaking on behalf of themselves, not God. When giving a prophetic word we need to leave room for people to test the word and hear from the Lord for themselves. We can overpower someone with an image of how we see ourselves or, even worse, flash the title of prophet so they are really intimidated. It does not mean you are a prophet just because you can hear a message from the Lord.

I love the metaphor Graham Cooke uses in his book *Developing Your Prophetic Gifting*: "Prophecy is like a swimming pool. There is a shallow end that all can safely use. . . . After the shallow end, there is a middle section where the water gets progressively deeper" (Chosen Books, 2003). Not everyone can tread water and be in the middle or even the deep end of the pool, but everyone can stand or sit in the shallow end of the pool. There is danger when someone who cannot swim tries to wade out and move to the deeper levels of the pool. They become a danger to themselves and to others.

I will not sugarcoat this for you. There are times when we can simply get it wrong. No one sets out to make a mistake, but it happens. How many times as parents have we gotten it wrong? We are acting from a heart of love, but we fail. What if our kids were allowed to stone us if we got it wrong or, worse yet, if they simply *thought* we got it wrong? I am fairly sure there would be a good number of us hiding out from our kids. The same is true with prophecy. There are times when we mean well, but we botch it. Therefore, if we are all to prophesy, we might want to go easy on the stoning.

As discussed in chapter 9, we often gloss over the responsibility to test prophecy, which rests on all of our shoulders. There is a responsibility on the part of the person who is delivering the word from the Lord, but the obligation does not stop there. The receivers of the word are directed to take what they are given before the Lord and ask God to reveal His heart. I think it is safe to assume that none of us wants to be wrong. I care about being accurate to the most annoying detail. The truth is I am human, so I miss it sometimes. When I do, I own up to it, ask forgiveness and move on.

Once while ministering during a conference setting I got it way wrong. I approached a couple who were sitting beside each other in the pew and began ministering to the husband. I said, "I see a picture of you sitting behind a desk. You are crunching numbers, and the ticker for the stock market is running across the bottom of the picture." I went on to share the word, "I also feel as if the Lord is saying you have this particular skill and talent." He said to me, "Nope, that's not me, but it is totally what my wife does for a living, and she's excellent at it." Awkward! Not only did I get it wrong, but I ministered to the wrong person entirely! My heart was in the right place but not directed at the right person.

I am so thankful we live under the covenant of grace and mercy. Not to mention we serve a God of second chances. (In the next chapter I am going to specifically address why we may get it wrong and what to do if that happens.)

So how do we trust, especially knowing people can get it wrong? It is essential we embrace the truth that God can call any one of us to provide guidance, insight and wisdom. If there is not a belief that there is a supernatural relationship between God and His people, then there is a bigger issue.

I am often asked, "Isn't that why God gave us the Bible? Isn't that enough?" It is true that the Bible is God-breathed (see 2 Timothy 3:16), infallible, unchangeable and is the standard by which prophetic words are measured. When God speaks prophetically it always lines up with His Word. It is also true that God gives us guidance through His Word and by speaking to us through His Holy Spirit, through Church leaders and through fellowship with others. If we embrace this truth, then we must acknowledge there is a place for the prophetic within today's Church. The Bible is our love letter from God; His Holy Spirit is what makes it a personal love letter to us.

Go Deeper

- When it comes to the gift of prophecy, how comfortable are you with receiving prophetic words from others? Very comfortable, sort of comfortable or uncomfortable? Why? What needs to happen for you to become more comfortable than you are?

- How comfortable are you with the idea of receiving prophetic words and sharing them with others? Very comfortable, sort of comfortable or uncomfortable? Why? What needs to happen for you to become more comfortable than you are?

- How does it make you feel to know that even well-intentioned people can get it wrong when it comes to hearing from the Lord? Take some time to ask the Holy Spirit to speak to you regarding what you just wrote.

- Ask the Holy Spirit this question and write out what you hear: What is the best way to deal with any sense of uncertainty or discomfort I may feel over knowing people can get it wrong?

Activation Prayer

God, help me step into the shallow end of the swimming pool and embrace the truths of Your Word. Guide me and show me where I have wrong thinking. Help me to operate in grace and mercy instead of in judgment of others.

Activate Encouragement

Which one of the following words resonates with or stands out most to you?

Hope	Strong	Path	Plans
Light	Peace	Destiny	Wisdom

Without looking at Scripture, can you think of any verses that might go with the specific word you chose? Write them out. Then use your Bible concordance or search function on your Bible app to find Scriptures that contain that word. Write them out on three-by-five-inch cards and ask God what other thoughts He would like to share. Next, ask the Holy Spirit to direct you to individuals who need encouragement pertaining to the Scriptures written on the card and then give them the card.

13

Missing the Mark

I have a mentor in my life whom I fondly refer to as Papa Carl. He is more than a spiritual father to me; he is the grandfather I never had. Carl is a man of God who has walked a hard road of persecution because of his prophetic gift, yet he is the biggest teddy bear you will ever meet. He has imparted wisdom and given guidance to me in some of my hardest times. He is also the person who taught me it is okay to open my mouth and speak.

When I first began to operate in the prophetic I was hesitant in stepping out to share. It was during this time that Papa Carl and I would get together weekly to minister and exercise our spiritual ears to hear God and speak encouragement to those around us. Carl has a powerful weapon in the form of a big, bony finger. He was not afraid to use this weapon and would frequently point it right in my face and with his deep voice say, "Debbie, just open your mouth and speak!" I learned not to sit near him, but it did not stop him.

For me, speaking aloud was a challenge. Early in life I was labeled a loudmouth, and speaking out always got me in trouble. As a self-defense mechanism I stopped opening my mouth.

My silence was how I skated undetected just below everyone's radar, and I became content in staying there. It worked. It was not that I did not have anything to say, but I had learned it was best to keep quiet.

Papa Carl once asked me, "Debbie, what's the worst thing that is going to happen if you open your mouth and speak?"

I thought about it for a moment and answered, "I could get it wrong, and that will lead to me getting into trouble. Also, what if someone took action based on something I got wrong? But the biggest reason is I don't like to be wrong! It is embarrassing to be wrong, not to mention I feel shameful."

He looked me in the eye and said, "You need to talk to Jesus about those things because He wants you to open your mouth and speak."

So I did. When I told God I did not want to open my mouth and speak, God simply said, *Don't you think I am big enough to cover any mess you make?*

Over the course of time I have learned several things from my fear of not wanting to speak out. I wanted to please people even at the expense of not pleasing God. I discovered that I lived my life based on fearing judgment from others rather than a reverent fear of God. I learned it is okay to get it wrong in the beginning. It is a learning process! Also, God is big, and if I simply stay humble as I operate in spiritual gifts and speak the words He gives me to share, He has my back. Last, I have discovered it is when I go beyond what He gives me to share or when I share my own opinion that I cross over the line and miss the mark.

Most individuals simply mishear because they lack experience. Hearing from God is exciting and something we should be stepping out to do. If you are unfamiliar with the ways of God, then you may not know what to do with what you get or you may not know how to begin. If that is you, be willing to step out and keep an attitude of humility. God wants us to encourage one another. When you stay in that mindset, how can it be wrong? I am sure you have heard this before, but my momma always told me, "If you can't say anything nice, then don't say anything at all." The same is true with speaking words of encouragement. The gift of prophetic encouragement will always have God's heart, which is love.

We can miss the mark too by viewing circumstances through our human lenses. Our lenses are, more often than not, flawed. There is no one person who is perfectly right one hundred percent of the time. When this happens, we can unwittingly misunderstand the interpretation or revelation God gives us. Remember: Shame is from the devil, but being embarrassed is a pride issue!

If I do not say what I think God wants me to say, then I am in disobedience to Him, and I will have to answer for it. Similarly, if I add more to what God gives me, then I have to answer for that too. I have also learned to avoid saying, "The Lord says," because it blocks a person's right to test or judge a word. Instead I say, "I feel impressed or prompted to share this with you; please pray over it and seek God's direction."

I am just a mouthpiece, a vessel God chooses to use. There are plenty of other people with willing hearts who would step out and encourage other people if I refuse or choose to misuse and abuse the privilege. Yes, we can choose to be disobedient or abuse prophecy, but are we willing to accept the consequences? What blessings would we be withholding from someone or ourselves if we chose to refuse God?

If someone is going to take action based on a word I gave or something I said, without seeking confirmation from the Lord, then that person is the one responsible for the choices that follow. That individual has as much of a responsibility to lay the word on the altar as I do to hear from God and seek His thoughts on the matter.

There is a fine line we walk when we operate in the gift of encouragement (prophecy). Just because it is a fine line does not

127

mean we should avoid it. We simply need to ask God to give us His heart to love others and grant us opportunities to use the gift of prophetic encouragement to bless others. We need not be fearful of speaking encouragement, strength or comfort to others. You may be asking yourself, *What do I do if I completely miss the mark?*

In order to answer this question, we must be mindful of where the fine line falls. In order to be set free and fully embrace God's gifts, we must first address some ways the enemy uses fear, doubt and unbelief to hinder us from walking in freedom. These struggles, when unaddressed, can lead to a variety of characteristics that significantly hinder our ability to exercise the prophetic gift of encouragement effectively:

- Inexperience

- Your own agenda
  » A word of observation or a word of instruction, despite good intentions, might represent your own opinion about the right way to handle a situation.
  » Speaking out of our own wisdom, albeit good counsel, cannot be represented as coming from the Lord.

- Pride and a know-it-all attitude
  » This heart attitude says, "Look at me! I am pretty important."
  » When people ask clarifying questions, this person gets defensive, as if no one should question his or her word.
  » This type of pride is an issue of the heart. It is characteristic of people who suffer from the idea that they are not capable of getting it wrong, and therefore, people should listen to them.

- Desire for title and recognition, which is always a matter of the heart

- Mindset that you are God's only mouthpiece
  - » This manifests as the type of pride that says you are good at what you do, so God does not need anyone else.
  - » It is an inflated sense of self-importance.

Have I mentioned I am not perfect? Oh, you're not either? Good! Then we can be friends. So from one friend to another, can I confess something? I had issues of wanting to be recognized. I have a history of people stealing my ideas and thoughts and passing them off as their own, and I wanted to be noticed. I want to be seen as having value and importance, don't you? Society tells us that in order to be seen, we must have a title and position. It is all in who you know and what title comes before your name or what letters come after your name. Thankfully, God both calls and equips us. He spent years working on my heart—sometimes gently, sometimes not so gently. He showed me that His recognition and the value He placed on me were more important than others' opinions.

Truthfully, the most important title ever is the one no one wants: servant. Jesus said that in order to be great, you must become small; in order to lead, we must first serve (see Matthew 20:26; Mark 9:35). Don't seek titles or recognition. Seek to be known by God. Seek to do the will of the Father, and partner with the Holy Spirit to speak words of encouragement to others.

Being God's mouthpiece is an honor and something we are all called to do. We are called to share His story. We are called to hear what He wants said and to speak it out without concern for others' recognition and without any sense of self-importance.

I have been around and in ministry with people who believed they were God's only mouthpiece. This is dangerous, and we must be careful. The root of this is pride as well. Pride is a pitfall that holds us back from entering the fullness of all God has for us.*

Giving and receiving a word are both subject to getting it wrong. Missing the mark can go two ways:

- You can get it wrong as a person who is giving a word.
- You can get it wrong as a receiver of the word.

It is possible for a person to give an accurate word of encouragement, but the receiver hears an entirely different message. I cannot tell you how many times I have seen this happen. In fact, my own husband, John, had this happen to him.

One time I brought John as a guest to my class for an exercise on activating encouraging words and an activation exercise on testing prophecy. One lady in the group said she saw how John liked fishing, but God was calling him to a higher calling, to become a fisher of men. He laughed and said, "Well, I do like to catch real fish, so I'll just stick with that."

At the time he was not a pastor, nor had he entertained thoughts of becoming one. He later told me the lady was way off base, and he had no desire to become a fisher of men. He took her word as encouragement that God was just pointing out something he liked to do and that God knew him. Fast-forward to today: We now pastor a church, and he is indeed a fisher of men.

This brings up more questions:

- How do we handle the relationship between the giving and receiving of the word when someone may get it wrong?
- How do we handle and act responsibly about it when either side misses the mark?
- Do we tell the other person they missed the mark and got it wrong?

*Feel free to refer back to the list of danger zones in chapter 11 for a more complete explanation of the result of pride in prophetic ministry.

I hope to answer these questions by sharing with you another testimony. Recently a man named John (not my husband) shared his need for prayer on Facebook regarding a prophetic word of encouragement he received while attending my class over nine years ago. In his request for prayer he shared that he had received a specific two-part message. One message had a timeline that John thought impossible, and consequently, he discounted the second part. At the time John thought his messenger had missed the mark. He explained:

> During one of the last activation times, we took turns ministering to one another. I was sitting in a circle with one of the guys, Mark, who always stood out to me. I recall him saying, "I'm unsure I can even hear God; this is really uncomfortable for me. I don't know if this even makes sense to you, but here's what I got." His first message was about my employment, and his impression was that I would be promoted by the end of the year. The second part was about my future spouse.

John discounted the word due to the work situation he was in. At the time of the word, it was the end of October, and a promotion was a stretch. John told God, "That's just not possible. My boss is going to have to go crazy or die for that to happen." John thought Mark had completely misheard and that nothing would come of it.

A little over a month after John received this prophetic encouragement, his boss experienced a car accident that forced her to resign her position. John was offered the promotion on December 31, and he began his new position January 1. John realized his messenger had not missed the mark.

John went on to share the second half of the encouraging word regarding his future bride:

> Recently I felt God prompt me to go back to the two-part message I received over nine years ago. I believe God gave me those

messages for a reason. One came to pass fairly quickly, blessing me, and the other I had to wait, trust and participate in. It still hasn't happened, but I believe it's in the works.

God was asking John to trust Him to bring it to pass, and John had to prepare himself for a relationship by receiving healing from his past. Lately he has been waiting on God for clarity for the second half of the message. When he questioned God about how long he was supposed to wait for a spouse, God asked him, *Just because it hasn't happened in your timing, why do you think it won't happen?*

There is a powerful lesson here. In the moments when we think someone got it wrong, it does not necessarily mean they did. I have always taught that if you get a word and it does not seem to fit or seems off the mark, set it aside and pray over it. Ask God to bring it to your memory if and when the time is right. If not, then move forward.

It is important to remember that a delay in the word's fruition does not make it wrong. Take Abram, for example. God told him he would be a father of nations when he was 75 years old. Years later, God returned to confirm and renew His promise. The time lapse between when God first spoke the promise and the fulfillment of His promise through Isaac's birth was a total of 25 years!

Do we need to tell the other person they got it wrong? It depends. What is the motive of your heart? Is it to put them in their place and let them know they got it wrong? I have had people do that to me. It does not feel good and is not valuable to anyone. When it happens I remind them they have a responsibility to take it to the Lord and ask Him, not just take my word for it. Here is a practical phrase to say that leaves space for grace: "Thank you for your encouragement, but it doesn't necessarily speak to me at this time; however, I will take it to the Lord and ask Him to confirm it."

I do talk with people who have a pattern of consistently missing the mark. I encourage them to go deeper with the Lord, discerning the ways He speaks to them by doing activation exercises. I also encourage them to ask God for confirmation in the small things before stepping out in bigger things.*

The bottom line is this: Do not let the fear of missing it stop you from stepping out. Understand that at some point you may get it wrong, but when you do, apologize. Having a heart of humility and grace makes all the difference. If you are speaking positive words of life and hope to others, they will be encouraged. And finally, God is big enough to fix any mistake you have made if you allow Him to.

Go Deeper

- Are you more afraid of failing, getting it wrong or being embarrassed? Ask God to show you your motives.

- Can you think of another story in Scripture in which there may have been a delay between the word that was spoken and when it came to pass?

- Is there a time you thought you were wrong and remained silent, only to find out the word God gave you was the right one after all?

Activation Prayer

Father God, help me to tune in to Your voice and hear You clearly. Help me have a heart of humility and show

---

*If you are interested in gaining some additional direction on this and other topics in this book, please visit my websites. Visit www.d2htraining.com to register for online classes and www.debbiekitterman.com for relevant articles about the prophetic and a calendar of my speaking schedule and upcoming events.

me if my lenses need to be adjusted in any way. I do not want the fear of missing the mark to hold me back from speaking encouragement to others. Give me boldness to step out and speak words of life.

Activate Encouragement

During your personal worship time or in church, ask God to give you a prophetic picture/vision. Make sure to write what God showed you and then specifically ask Him what He is speaking to you or showing you. Also look for Scriptures that will go with the picture/vision you received.

Be prepared to encourage someone else by sharing what God revealed to you so both of you can be encouraged.

Think on It!

When I receive messages for individuals, especially leaders, I ask the Lord, "Is this a word for me to deliver, or is this a word of knowledge for me to pray and intercede for the individual?" If I am to deliver it, that is exactly what I do. Once the word has been delivered, it is not mine to pick up again or agonize over. It is their job to do with it as the Lord leads them.

Think about it this way: Getting messages of encouragement is like being a mail carrier. God has given you something to deliver; that is your job. It is not the mailman's job to come back and make sure the recipient paid his or her bills or responded to the letters. The mail carrier solely delivers the mail.

I will admit this is easier said than done. I have experienced what it is like to give specific words to people who go on to do nothing with those words. Once I gave a message to a pastor who was retiring and his successor. The Lord spoke a clear, encouraging word about the church coming to a crossroads and what they needed to do moving forward. I emailed the message to both pastors, and I got an immediate response from the pastor transitioning out. He loved it and thought it was right on and asked if he could share it on Sunday. My response was simple: "It is your word now; you can do as you see fit."

That Sunday the word was never shared, and while I wondered why, I knew it was not mine to question. Later I found out that one pastor loved it and the other did not. I did exactly what God asked me to do: I humbly submitted the word. The rest was up to them to walk it out—or not.

Remember my friend Bob, who was on staff at a church? During our times of mentoring I often gave activations, just like I have included in this book. This particular time the activation was to ask God the name of a specific individual and then ask God for a word of encouragement. Here is what Bob shared with me:

> As I asked God for a name to pray for, I got "Matt." I said, "Okay, what do You want me to pray for?" Immediately I got the words

extraordinary grace and *treasure trove of wisdom*. God shared what I considered to be a great, encouraging word.

I delivered the word in person to Matt with a disclaimer I could be off, so he would also need to take it before God. Although Matt did not verbally agree with or confirm this word, he was quite gracious about it. I felt he was letting me down gently by saying it was okay to miss it and to keep practicing. It was a rather weird experience, since I knew enough about recent situations in his life to sense that it was on target. It was just another opportunity for me to learn to give the word and then let God do the rest, because it's not up to me.

Another friend had a similar experience. She shared two words with a pastor and missionary she had known for years, but he did not seem pleased to hear it.

First, I saw a picture of Pastor and the outline of Africa. He was standing in a pair of oversized, well-worn logging boots that were planted deeply in the soil. Pastor stood securely in the boots even though the shoelaces weren't tied. The boots were firmly planted in the soil, allowing him to step in or out without stumbling. All around him were old-fashioned oil wells, which represented wealth. He appeared happy.

Next, I saw churches and heard the Lord say, *At times it will seem effortless for you. This is a new work, but it is not a pioneering work.* I interpreted that the soil had been prepared, and now the wealth was going to come up just like an oil well.

I barely finished sharing the word when he got in my face and said, "You are messing with my life, young lady," and walked off. Horrified, I scurried home to pray. Later I heard the Lord say, *Write out the message and give it to him.* So I did obediently.

The next day I humbly approached him and apologized if I had offended him, but I knew he needed this message. He accepted the message indifferently. Although I felt peace, this interaction still bothered me for years.

Nine years later there was an announcement that Pastor was stepping out of the church and into a regional supervisor position over churches in many African countries! I laughed and cried out of relief when I heard the news. I had heard and obeyed in faith, but it was not my job to make it happen.

Activation Prayer

Lord, help me just to be the mail carrier and not get offended when I get a word for someone and they do not receive it. Lord, help me to remember it is my job to pray or share about what You give me, but it is their responsibility to walk it out.

Go Deeper

- What safeguards need to be in place before giving a word of encouragement?

- Do you think sharing a prophetic word of encouragement with leadership is harder than sharing encouragement with someone else? Why do you think that is?

- What are some practical ways you can ensure that you are only the deliverer of the word and not the enforcer?

- How can you stay positive and encouraged when those around you are negative and discouraging? What does Scripture have to say?

- Read 1 Peter 4:10–11. Does this truth make it easier to encourage others?

14

Circle of Trust:
Being Submitted, Committed
and Connected

One of my spiritual mentors gave me a pivotal piece of advice that has served as a cornerstone of my ministry. It is also a vital word of caution to anyone operating in spiritual gifts, especially the prophetic. He said, "It is essential that prophetic individuals be submitted, committed and connected."

It has taken me several years to grasp the full meaning of his words. At first I did not understand the enormity of his statement because I did not understand the prophetic as a whole. I had no idea of the value of being connected and submitted since I was very naïve about the nature of the prophetic environment.

The Church is the Bride of Christ, and we need to love each other and be submitted, committed and connected to one another. I know the Church is not perfect, but God does not want us running off to do our own thing when we cannot have it our way either. We need each other, yet we have a natural tendency to isolate ourselves, thus hindering the prophetic and the entire Church. A body was meant to function with all its parts working together in harmony with love toward one another. This cannot happen when parts of the body go missing. We must build relationships based on trust. We must work together and utilize the God-given gifts we have been given. When we do we will bring heaven to earth, creating an environment where people can meet Jesus on a personal level.

Submitted

There are many Scriptures throughout the New Testament that talk about submission (see 1 Peter 2:13; 5:5; James 4:7; Ephesians 5:21–24; Hebrews 13:17). Still, yielding ourselves to God is hard, which is why some never get saved. Their view of God is one of submission and authority in its most negative sense. Submission is a heart attitude, which includes a willingness to yield to Him and to the spiritual counselors He has placed in our life. No matter how much we might dislike the word, Scripture is clear we are to be submitted to one another. Ephesians 5:21 admonishes us, "Submit to one another out of reverence for Christ," and Proverbs 12:15 counsels, "The way of fools seems right to them, but the wise listen to advice."

At my husband's work they have a policy called Disagree and Commit. It means that every person on the team voices his or her opinions and arguments to the team leader. Then the leader takes each perspective under careful consideration and makes a decision. Once the decision is announced, all fully commit their support, regardless of their previous position. The same must be true in the Kingdom of God.

Submission to one another is especially important in the prophetic. We need to be accountable to each other to speak and receive the truth in love. I know it is vitally important that

I be submitted to trusted advisors in leadership. Just because I have a gifting of prophecy does not mean I am viewing it correctly. Submitting my perspective keeps me balanced and prevents me from becoming a lone wolf.

Prophets must have other prophetic people in their lives they can submit themselves to—not to be in positions of power but to be a peer in a position of trust. King David was a prophet (see Acts 2:29–30), but God sent him two prophets, Nathan and Gad, to provide him wise counsel (see 1 Samuel 22:5; 2 Samuel 12; 24:11–25; 1 Kings 1:11–45; 1 Chronicles 21:9).

When we are submitted to one another, we are unified. We do not have to agree, but we must support and strengthen one another.

Committed

Today we live in a culture in which people do not honor their commitments. There was a time when our words were considered a binding contract, but not anymore. We can say something and mean it at the time, but when we change our mind or something better comes along, suddenly it is okay to quit. We have adopted the idea that commitments are temporary. These short-lived commitments run rampant in relationships, jobs and churches.

If you are a parent, I am sure you will relate to this story: We went through a season of sport hopping with both of our children. They would play a sport just long enough to find out they didn't like it when things got tough or when they were no longer having fun. Then the complaining would begin. It was often, "The coach isn't fair," or, "I'm not getting to play." They would whine, saying they wanted to quit. Anticipating the tough road ahead each time they expressed a desire to switch to a new sport, we counseled our children to think seriously about it before making the commitment to join. We were always clear that once they made the decision they would have to see it through to the end of the season.

For several years my daughter was involved with competitive gymnastics. She reached a point where she was tired and wanted to be done. I told her I supported her decision, but she was obligated to finish out the season. Then she could hang up her leotard. She did not understand why she could not quit right then. She protested long and hard. Her father and I explained she had made a commitment to her team and her coach, and she needed to see it to the end. It was really tough, but at our insistence she stuck it out.

As a parent, I would like to believe these experiences matured my kids and that one day they will thank me for it. I will let you all know when it happens! For now, we get to hear about how tough we are and how she will certainly never do that to her kids. We shall see.

My point is this: When problems arise in the church—and they *always* arise—instead of having a conversation with a leader, people often hop to the next church hoping they have left the problem behind. It is no surprise when the problems follow them to the new church, so they are forced to move again. These are people who love Jesus but struggle with making a commitment to His Bride.

Jesus asks that we commit to one another fully (see Ephesians 4:32). Remember in the Scriptures when Jesus told Peter things would get tough in the coming hours and days? Jesus told him, "You are going to deny Me." Shocked, Peter adamantly refuted what Jesus was telling him. Later, when Jesus was captured, tried and sentenced to crucifixion, a fearful Peter denied knowing Him three times to complete strangers. When the going got tough, Peter ran away both spiritually and physically. I can only imagine his anguish when he recognized his failure.

After Jesus was resurrected, Peter, thinking he had failed and was unworthy to be called a disciple of Christ, went back to his old vocation. In John 21 we see Peter fishing on a boat. Scripture records they caught nothing all night. Then early the next morning a man they did not recognize called to them from the shore and asked if they had caught anything. He told them to cast their nets to the right side of the boat. They followed His instruction and caught a great number of fish. John realized who it was and said aloud, "It is the Lord." Peter wrapped his garments around himself and immediately jumped out of the boat and waded to the shore. His desire to see his friend Jesus is apparent. The enemy would have loved nothing more than to keep Peter feeling separated from Him. But Jesus is about restoration!

God knew the plans He had for Peter. He was called to be a fisher of men! Peter was filled with the Spirit of God and spoke with authority and power, all because Jesus honored His commitment to Peter in his moment of weakness. Just as Jesus restored Peter, He wants to restore relationship and fulfill His promises within each one of us. There are times when I have wholeheartedly committed to a path, only to abandon it when it became too hard. I can relate to Peter, can't you?

When we do not honor our commitments to one another, the door is open for the enemy to deposit shame, condemnation, rejection and fear, separating us from one another.

Connected

We are built for relationship with God and each other. Scripture is clear: We need to be connected with one another. Still, there are times I feel spiritually used up and fight the impulse to withdraw. I am not talking about recharging my batteries. Even Jesus did this. I am talking about pulling away from my support system.

By nature I am a positive, joyful person. I love God, and I love people. In fact, the first prophetic word I ever received said I was like a pendulum swinging back and forth between loving God and loving people. In the past, however, I found myself feeling disconnected and isolated. I was running from writing this book and filling my hours with busy work. The insignificant details provided a distraction and kept me from accomplishing the very thing God had told me to do.

So what is the fix when we sense this happening? The first step is recognizing that it is happening and then taking steps to reconnect. I know when I isolate myself I am a sitting duck. My first defense is to circle my spiritual wagons and stand within the safety of my faith, family and friends.

Isolation is where the enemy likes to corner us, twisting the truth and whispering lies. We are all part of one body, functioning together (see 1 Corinthians 12:12; Romans 12:4). In the gospels we see Jesus being led by the Spirit into the wilderness after His baptism. Jesus was alone, disconnected and tempted for forty days and forty nights. The passages in Matthew and Luke tell us Satan came and tempted Jesus three separate times. Each time Jesus quoted the truth of the Scriptures back to him. After the third assault Satan withdrew in defeat, and angels of the Lord were sent to minister to Jesus' needs.

In the Garden of Eden the entire conversation between Eve and the serpent is the perfect illustration of Satan's twisted truth. It only happened because Eve was alone and separated from Adam and God. The enemy's tactics never change. He wants to separate us from God and from one another, to isolate us. In the isolation of doubt and unbelief we risk broken relationship with God. It is this lie of the enemy that hinders the development of our character and holds us in bondage.

Jesus was victorious because He was submitted, committed and connected to the Word and to His Father. That is why it is no less important for us to remember that "it is essential that prophetic individuals be submitted, committed and connected." Jesus says He will never leave us or forsake us, no matter what.

Go Deeper

- Would you say you have a problem submitting to leadership? Would others say you have a problem submitting?

- What image or thoughts come to mind when you hear the word *commitment*?

- Why is it important to stay connected? What does Scripture say about it?

Activation Prayer

God, help me to recognize my need for connection. Alert me to when I am isolating myself from You and others. Show me if there are attitudes or hurts in me that need to be healed so I may fully walk in forgiveness and the plans You have for me. Forgive me for the areas in my life where I have not been submitted, committed or connected to You. Help me to understand that I am blessed and strengthened when I am in community with others.

Activate Encouragement

Write a list of at least five to ten people who are in your inner circle. Then assess where you are in being submitted to, committed to or connected with them. Ask the Lord how He wants to reestablish or move forward in your life concerning these relationships.

Encouragement in Action

Gill Man

Several years ago I ministered to a group of leaders and pastors at a church in California. As I finished ministering to the people sitting at the first table, one of the ladies caught my attention and asked if I would come back and minister to her husband, Mike. It is hard to admit, but at the time I was flattered that she was specifically seeking me out to minister to someone close to her.

When he arrived, his wife came and got me. It was clear he was more than reluctant to participate. Mike stood over six feet tall, like a football linebacker. He proceeded to cross his arms and plant his feet like he was bracing himself for a fight. His stance sent a clear message. As I started to pray over him, I asked the Lord to share a word of encouragement with me. I kept seeing this truly bizarre picture. The image was the creature from the black lagoon as he came out of the water. I had been feeling pretty full of myself before Mike and his wife arrived for ministry, and it seemed clear to me that God was giving me a swift dose of humility. Unfortunately, my knee-jerk reaction was to focus more on my own discomfort than on sharing the message I was receiving for Mike. As I continued to minister I was still only seeing a picture of this creature, which in my mind would certainly fail to impress Mike. I tried praying harder. Nothing. *Nada.*

I stopped and looked up at Mike, who really did tower over me. I did not want to sound like a complete idiot, so I contemplated telling him I was not getting anything. But that felt even more embarrassing. My voice was barely a whisper. "I am not sure what I am supposed to do with this picture. I keep asking God to give me something else, but He's not. You may think it's crazy, but perhaps it will mean something to you." I shared a picture from the movie and the words I kept hearing: "gill man." I braced myself and slowly asked again if this meant anything to him.

I was dumbfounded when he quickly said, "Yes, it does." He communicated he always associated our walk with Jesus as being like that of a "gill man." As he spoke, his entire demeanor began to soften. He went on to explain that our relationship with Jesus should be like a fish, which is immersed completely in the water and survives by breathing water in and out through its gills. He compared the water to Jesus and our relationship with Him. We should be completely immersed in Him, breathing Him in and out daily.

Honestly, I was more amazed than Mike. Who would have thought a word so bizarre was really from God? In this experience I doubted God and His blessing on my life because I allowed my ego to take center stage instead of trusting Him.

I would like to say that I do not struggle with doubt today, but the truth is I do, especially when God has a habit of showing me the craziest pictures, like the toast and jam story I told in chapter 4.

I ministered at a women's retreat, and a lady ministering on another team was sharing with me how embarrassed she was by the word God gave her. I tilted my head, intrigued to hear more. Donna said, "Debbie, it was awful. All I got was the word *pancake*! I mean, what in the world do you say about a pancake? I kept thinking, *This can't be God*. When it was my turn to minister I blurted out, 'All I'm getting is *pancake*!'"

I chuckled a little at Donna because I could relate so well. God was indeed speaking to her, and "pancake" meant something specific and special to the woman receiving the word.

We need to remember attitude is everything, and so is the condition of our heart. We must be willing to set aside our pride and let God shine. Truthfully, we must trust Him. He knows what He is doing.

Activation Prayer

Lord, give me an attitude adjustment where I need one and continually check the condition of my heart so that it is in tune with Yours. May I too be a "gill man" for Jesus, breathing You in and being completely immersed in You daily.

Go Deeper

- Why is a healthy heart attitude important?

- Have you ever let your ego take center stage? Write about it.

15

The Perfect Example

The focus of this book is the spiritual gift of prophecy as it is portrayed in the New Testament, which is rooted in encouragement. It is not on the Old Testament story of prophets and foretelling. God wants to communicate with us the same way He did with Jesus when He walked on earth. Jesus' relationship with the Father is prophecy in action: "The testimony of Jesus is the spirit of prophecy" (Revelation 19:10 NASB). When we experience the same kind of relationship that Jesus did, we open ourselves up to receive all kinds of mysteries and revelations from the Father. As Paul wrote in 1 Corinthians 2:9–10 (NLT), "No eye has seen, no ear has heard, and no mind has imagined what God has prepared for those who love him."

In order to understand fully the importance of prophecy in Jesus' earthly life we need to understand equally the other ministry functions of evangelist, pastor, teacher and apostle. These ministries, called the fivefold ministries, are gifts meant to work in harmony. Much like the human body, they do not operate successfully by themselves. The unity of believers, working together in relationship with one another, is vital to the health of the entire body. These ministry functions, as modeled by Jesus, are the perfect illustration of a vital and healthy life.

These ministries are not titles or offices. When our desire is to label these gifts with titles, we make it about status and position. Keep in mind that the fivefold ministries Paul teaches about in 1 Corinthians focus on unity and maturity and are God-appointed:

> *Christ himself gave* the apostles, the prophets, the evangelists, the pastors and teachers, to equip his people for works of service, so that the body of Christ may be built up until we all reach *unity in the faith and in the knowledge of the Son of God and become mature, attaining to the whole measure of the fullness of Christ.*
>
> Ephesians 4:11–13, emphasis added

> There are different kinds of gifts, but the same Spirit distributes them. There are different kinds of service, but the same Lord. There are different kinds of working, but *in all of them and in everyone* it is the same God at work. *Now to each one the manifestation of the Spirit is given for the common good.*
>
> 1 Corinthians 12:4–7, emphasis added

Apostle

The word *apostle* in Greek means "one sent forth" as an ambassador of the Gospel.* Jesus' entire life was about showing us how to live. He was sent forth to pay for our sins so that we might have eternal life and a relationship with Him, the Father and the Holy Spirit. His life was a model for truth, hope, love, grace, peace and much more. Jesus is referred to as an apostle in Hebrews 3:1: "Therefore, holy brothers and sisters, who share

---

*Definition quoted from *Thayer's Greek Lexicon*, accessed at Biblehub.com.

in the heavenly calling, fix your thoughts on Jesus, whom we acknowledge as our apostle and high priest."

It is important to point out there is a difference between an apostle and a disciple. Many people confuse the two. A disciple is someone who follows the teachings of Jesus, sharing the good news. An apostle raises up disciples, much like Jesus did with the original Twelve and Paul with Timothy. We are called to be both, but we must begin as disciples. We may not have a calling upon our life like Paul, but we are to be apostle-like in the way we live our lives. We have all been commissioned by Jesus to go make disciples: "Therefore go and make disciples of all nations, baptizing *them in the name of the Father and of the Son and of the Holy Spirit*" (Matthew 28:19, emphasis added).

Jesus sent us forth. He told us to go and share about Him. Does this mean we are all called to carry the label of apostle? No! It means whatever God has given to you as your job—whether it is driving a taxicab or teaching school—you are sent forth as an ambassador to live your life as a reflection of Him.

Evangelist

The word *evangelist* means "bringer of good news."* Simply put, an evangelist is someone who tells the good news of Jesus Christ and proclaims the Gospel. Jesus was an evangelist. Wherever Jesus went, a crowd would gather to hear Him speak. His words gave hope and pointed the people toward heaven. Jesus told His disciples, "I must proclaim the good news of the kingdom of God to the other towns also, because that is why I was sent" (Luke 4:43).

Jesus commissioned the disciples to go and spread the Good News: "And then he told them, 'Go into all the world and preach the Good News to everyone'" (Mark 16:15 NLT). We have also

*Definition quoted from *Strong's Concordance*, accessed at Biblehub.com.

been given the commission to spread the Good News. When many of us hear the word *evangelist*, we think of a person like Billy Graham. Does this mean we are to hold huge revivals? No, it means we are instructed to share what Jesus has done for us and how He has changed our lives. We are all called to live our lives in such a way that we direct people toward heaven, giving them hope for today. Evangelism is simple: Tell your story of how Jesus changed your life for the better.

Pastor/Shepherd

The Greek word used for *pastor* also means "shepherd."* Shepherds tend and protect the sheep within their care. Likewise, a pastor is called to tend, feed and protect the people within his or her church. In the book of Acts, Paul addresses the elders in Ephesus when he refers to the people within their care as the "flock" and them as "shepherds":

> Keep watch over yourselves and all the flock of which the Holy Spirit has made you overseers. Be shepherds of the church of God, which he bought with his own blood.
>
> Acts 20:28

Jesus was a pastor to the disciples. In fact, John 10:1–21 outlines how Jesus described Himself as the good Shepherd: "I am the good shepherd. The good shepherd lays down his life for the sheep" (verse 11).

When we think about the role of a pastor, we automatically look to the church. We think of the pastor as the person in charge of running the church or as the individual who preaches on Sunday. However, God has also called us to be pastors within our circle of influence. This includes our families, neighbors,

---

*Definition quoted from *Strong's Concordance*, accessed at Biblehub.com.

co-workers and even strangers who cross our paths. How do we pastor them?

When Jesus sat with the woman at the well and spoke to her He showed He cared. He spoke truth and life to her. More importantly, He showed her how to continue in His footsteps. In John 21:15–18 Peter was reinstated after he denied ever knowing Jesus. Jesus emphasized that if Peter truly loved Him, then he was to take care of His sheep (the people). The same applies to us. If we love Jesus, we are called to love and shepherd His people.

Teacher

A teacher, or rabbi, was an instructor acknowledged for his mastery in his field of learning. As teachers of the Law, rabbis used their knowledge and skill of teaching for more than just simply preaching. As teachers, they were also to be daily, living examples of how to live through behaviors and actions. The ability to preach does not make someone a teacher, nor does being a teacher make someone a good preacher.

Jesus was a wonderful and gifted teacher (see John 3:2). Even people who rejected Him as the Son of God believed He was a teacher. Let me state clearly: Jesus was sent by God to live life as a man to model how to live. As we read the New Testament we see that Jesus taught through sharing His Father's wisdom and through His actions in daily living.

Prophet

The meaning of the word *prophet* in Greek is "one who speaks forth messages from God."* So what is the role of prophecy in our lives? Jesus said, "I only say what the Father tells me to

*Definition paraphrased from *HELPS Word-studies*, accessed at Biblehub.com.

say and do what the Father shows me to do." He was listening, hearing and obeying (see John 5:19; 8:28; 10:27; 12:49–50). Just as Jesus modeled the five functions of ministry, we are called to model Him. Our first step is to hear from the Father, as Jesus did. This is the role of prophecy in our lives.

We have all been called to go forth, evangelize, pastor, teach and prophesy to those within our realm of influence. We are not all called to be pastors or evangelists, but we can all pastor and evangelize within our communities. Everyone has been given portions of the five functions, and just as Jesus did, we are called to serve.

> But you are a chosen people, a royal priesthood, a holy nation, God's special possession, that you may declare the praises of him who called you out of darkness into his wonderful light.
>
> 1 Peter 2:9

Go Deeper

- As you read Revelation 19:10, what does it speak/mean to you?

- Which fivefold ministry attribute would you say is your strongest? Why?

- Which one is your weakest? Why? How can you strengthen it in your life?

Activation Prayer

Jesus, I acknowledge that You lived Your life here on earth to serve as a perfect example for me. I recognize that each of the fivefold functions operated in Your life. Help me to be well rounded and to develop all the ministry functions in my own life so that they can be released within my circle of influence. Lord, bring balance where there is imbalance and strengthen areas of weakness in my life. Encourage me to step out and be prophecy in action.

Activate Encouragement

Before you leave the house, ask the Lord if there is anyone you will meet who needs encouragement. He may give you a name, a description or a location where someone will be. Take time to pray over what He gives you and how He wants you to encourage that individual.

If you do not receive a specific person or word at that time, try the following as an alternative activity, and then at another time try the one above again. Turn to the Activate Encouragement section at the end of chapter 12 and choose one of the words listed there. Once you have chosen a word from the list, ask God to give you an encouraging word related to your choice and also a verse to go with it. Write it out and carry it with you until you feel prompted by the Holy Spirit to give it to a specific individual.

16

Working Together

While each of us exhibits tendencies toward certain portions of the five ministry callings, there are individuals whom God specifically calls to be an apostle, prophet, evangelist, pastor or teacher. These are positions they have been called to hold in the Church.

The New Testament is God's letter and instruction given to inspire us toward the common goal of winning souls, growing people to maturity and being in relationship with the Father and each other. As with most things in the New Testament, you can follow it back to its roots in the Old Testament. Why? Because God, in His sovereignty, already had a plan for the way things were to work. The Old Testament and New Testament have many theological parallels. Just as Moses was a deliverer to God's chosen people, the Israelites, Jesus is the Deliverer for all people.

Moses was never meant to do everything by himself. He was given a job to do: lead God's people out of Egypt into the Promised Land. Moses was to lead, prepare and equip the Israelites for the next season of life. Moses tried to be all things to all people, but he burned out. At that time he was the only one who knew how to do the job, but it quickly became obvious he needed help.

In Exodus 18:14–27 we see Moses' father-in-law, Jethro, giving Moses sound advice: Find others who are capable and teach them what you know and what God has shown you. Then release them to sit in judgment over the people and the lesser cases (see Exodus 18:19–23). Moses listened to his advice and established a court to hear and judge the issues people brought to him.

God does not intend for any of us to carry our burdens alone. He chooses to partner with us by gifting each of us with different skills, talents and abilities. On our own, we are not complete. We are created to work together so we may function as one body. How many times have you tried to be all things to all people? I have done it, and it is exhausting. It is not only difficult, it is impossible.

In the book of Acts we read how community life is supposed to work. We see how everyone did his or her part by working together in the early church. No one clamored for position or recognition; instead, they worked in unity. They each brought their skills and talents to the table, showing respect and honor for one another.

Many biblical scholars believe the list in Ephesians 4:11 is more than a list of titles. They interpret it as a chain of authority with apostles and prophets being at the top, followed next by evangelists, pastors and finally teachers. They believe this because of 1 Corinthians 12:27–28, where Paul talks about one body with many parts:

> Now you are the body of Christ, and each one of you is a part of it. And God has placed in the church first of all apostles, second prophets, third teachers, then miracles, then gifts of healing, of helping, of guidance, and of different kinds of tongues.

God's design, however, is for the Church to work together as a team. There needs to be relationship and an openness to hear what each has to say. In Ephesians 4:1–16 Paul reveals how unity is always God's intended structure for the Church. God gave prophets to the Church so they could bring the message from Him to others. Prophets can see what God is trying to accomplish and help direct or redirect as necessary. A pastor's job is to love, protect and ensure the people are cared for. A pastor, unless he is doubly gifted, cannot do the job of a prophet, and vice versa.

Sadly, we do not always see the Church working together. It is not uncommon today to see leaders competing with one another. Everyone wants control. Some are territorial and jealous and do not want their members to stray to other churches. Unfortunately, the trend is to focus more on statistics and numbers and less on actual individuals. The truth is, churches need members in order to function and operate. The focus should not be on how big or small a church body is; it should be on what God is asking of the church. What vision has God given you or your church, and how can you work together to accomplish it?

There are churches that operate as God intended. What do these churches have that others do not? Teamwork! They honor one another and work together. They have a depth of relationship with one another and with God. They have developed trust and promote each other over themselves. They listen to and defer to one another (see Romans 12:3 NASB; Philippians 2:3–4; 1 Corinthians 9:19; 12:25–27; Colossians 3:12–13, just to mention a few). They love one another and are committed to the body of Christ. Are there people in charge of these churches who clearly make the decisions? Yes, but they are also willing to listen and take input. They have been given respect not solely because of their position but more so because of how they treat those around them.

With the disciples, Jesus was clearly their leader. He taught them, loved them, listened to them and corrected them when needed. Most surprising, Jesus included the disciples in the process. When He multiplied the loaves and fishes He gave them opportunity to participate in the miracle—hands on. Jesus honored them, and they honored Him.

There are many churches that desire to equip their members to hear from God. They want them activated and operating in the spiritual gift of prophecy in a healthy way. I have had the honor of working with different churches to train and equip their body of believers to hear from God and operate in the prophetic gift of encouragement.

Recently I had the privilege of taking a Hispanic congregation through an eight-week course designed to teach them how to flow in the spiritual gift of prophecy. While it had its own pastors and leaders, this congregation was under the umbrella of a larger, English-speaking congregation. Upon arriving the first night to teach, not only did I have the Hispanic congregation, but I also had individuals from the English-speaking congregation as well. I loved it! I asked the pastor of the Hispanic church how it came to be that one-third of the class did not know how to speak Spanish. I asked if they attended his congregation. He responded, "No. During our joint staff meeting I mentioned to the entire staff I was going to have you come teach my congregation on how to hear from God, so word got out."

Evidently, this was the first time since he had been there that an activity like this brought these two congregations together. His next words struck me as truth but were also prophetic in nature. He said, "Debbie, you are a bridge between the nations." For those eight weeks it was powerful to watch the blending of those two congregations. Though they were meeting in the same building, they had been separated by culture until their common desire to grow in the things of God brought them together to learn and mature alongside one another.

This is what God intends for all His believers. It is not about church buildings or programs, though these are necessary; it is about building the Kingdom of God here on the earth. He wants us to work together. We are on the same team with the purpose of going and telling the story of what Jesus has done for us.

The Great Commission is to share the good news of Jesus Christ with everyone. It will not come about by one or two individuals. It is essential we all do our part to use our skills and talents together for the common good.

Go Deeper

- How would you describe the model for the New Testament church as found in the book of Acts?

- How is your church specifically following the outline in Scripture?

- In what areas could the modern-day Church improve?

- Why is unity important in the Church? Provide a Scripture to substantiate your answer.

Activation Prayer

Lord Jesus, work in my heart and the hearts of those who believe in You. Help us to honor one another. Help us not to be in competition with one another. Instead, let us be open toward one another and come together in unity and love.

Activate Encouragement

Look in the Bible and find one person from the Old Testament and one person from the New Testament who line up with each of the five ministry functions. Now identify individuals you know personally who fulfill each of these five offices. (Keep in mind they may not be employed by the church.)

Think on It!

Oooh, Shiny!

The prophetic is like a bunch of presents under a Christmas tree all wrapped in brown paper, except one. This one is wrapped in the most enticing, shiny paper and adorned with sparkling ribbons. It is the super special gift everybody wants. This desire creates every sort of human vice. Isn't it ironic that the gift for all is the one people want to own exclusively? I believe God has revealed the reason why. One night while reading 1 Corinthians 14, something very subtle caught my attention:

> I would like every one of you to speak in tongues, but I would rather have you prophesy. *The one who prophesies is greater than the one who* speaks in tongues, unless someone interprets, so that the church may be edified.
>
> 1 Corinthians 14:5, emphasis added

"The one who prophesies *is greater than* the one who . . ." When I read the Scripture this particular time those ten words slapped me in the face. Could this be why there is such a problem?

No question, there is something in all of us that wants to be recognized. The better question, then, is this: Is there also something in all of us that is crying out to be "greater than"? It reminds me of Lucifer vying to share power with God. Just as he twisted the truth in Eden, the enemy still twists the truth today. His ultimate goal is to diminish the gift of prophecy. He plants seeds of self-importance in a way that makes us move away from God's intended plan for this incredible gift. When Jesus was in the desert, Satan tried to tempt Him with the desire for recognition and status, but Jesus was not buying it, and we should not either.

Activation Prayer

Dear Jesus, help me find my recognition and self-worth in You, not in what I do or what others think about me. Shape me into Your likeness and help me to withstand the temptation of the enemy. I long to be more like You, Jesus, in all I say and do. I want this powerful gift to operate in my life according to Your intended plan for me.

Go Deeper

- When you think of the prophetic gift of encouragement, what picture comes to mind?

- How does this picture influence the way you perceive the gift of prophetic encouragement?

- Now that you have read this book, has your perception changed about prophecy? If so, how?

- Why do you think Paul says in 1 Corinthians 14:5 that the one who prophesies is greater?

17

It's Not about Me

On May 1, 2010, in the middle of the night I heard God speak these words: *The misuse and abuse of prophecy inside and outside the Church has to stop!* There was a particular emphasis on those last three words, "has to stop."

Helicopter Dream

> I am flying in a helicopter, and I have the sense that Jesus is with me. I can't see Him, but I know He is there. He's piloting the helicopter, surveying the land and pointing out landmarks. I am captivated by what I see and do not want to miss anything. I feel the excitement pulse through my body. All of a sudden Jesus tilts the helicopter forward in a nosedive so I can get a better view. My heart is in my throat; I am not prepared. Thick, black smoke is billowing from the ground, indicative of a war-torn land. It looks like a scene from an apocalyptic movie. The terrain and atmosphere have suddenly changed from thrill and wonder to one of death and desolation. I am jarred awake.

I first shared this dream over twelve years ago with a group of close friends. We asked God for His interpretation. After a lot of prayer we concluded that Jesus was revealing a perspective of events within the spiritual realm. Sometimes we do not receive the full revelation of what God is trying to tell us until it is the appropriate time. That was the case with this dream.

While writing this book I was having lunch with Papa Carl, and he asked, "Did you ever figure out what the Lord was trying to tell you about the helicopter dream?" I had not thought about it in ages, and I was curious why he was asking. "I'm not sure," Carl responded, "but I think it's important. It has something to do with the book God asked you to write."

Carl readily admits he struggles with his memory, so for him to remember my dream of more than twelve years previous was totally a God thing! I heard the Lord whisper to my heart:

I was preparing you for this moment. It's time! It's time for you to share what I have placed in you. . . . It's time for you to reveal the things you've seen and experienced. I said it then, and I am saying it again: The misuse and abuse of prophecy inside and outside the Church has to stop! Write the book!

As God spoke those words to my heart, the image of the dream played over in my mind. A war is being waged over the gifts of the Spirit, which include prophecy. Why is this simple act such a battlefield? Why is there so much misuse and abuse? You might want to pour yourself another cup of coffee, as this is not a simple question with a tidy answer.

The abuse of prophecy is rooted in the human need for power and control. In simple terms, the act of prophecy is hearing and retelling the very heart and mind of God. What greater power could there be? Whether it is a one-line email that is carelessly delivered untested or a full-scale assault designed to hijack a church body, the action of relaying God's plan in the absence of truth is manipulation and can lead to devastating spiritual injury. The danger is further magnified with technology and thin relationships providing the perfect cover.

The prophetic is intended to draw people into a closer and deeper relationship with God. In many cases, however, it is not allowed to function properly. Some have used prophecy for personal gain with disastrous results. I have met several of those who have been affected. These wounds are deep and hard to heal. I do not think it can be overstated: It is wrong to use prophecy or any other gift of the Spirit for personal gain.

Pam has a story of when a trusted friend purposely misused confidential information and passed it off as prophetic knowledge. Finally, with the advice of godly counsel, Pam got the courage to leave an abusive relationship. For her safety, this also meant leaving her home church of sixteen years. Pam reached out to her friend, who was also the women's ministry leader, to forewarn her of Pam's decision to leave. Pam asked her friend to keep this to herself, but the leader did otherwise.

Next Sunday morning her husband came home visibly angry. The elders of the church had pulled him aside and told him the women's ministry leader had received a word from the Lord that his wife was leaving. Pam told me, "How ironic. The Lord gave her the exact same 'word' that I'd shared in confidence." It was a lie that caused hurt to the woman in the abusive relationship, but it caused this church leader seemingly to look good and gain a reputation as being someone who could hear from God.

I have heard similar stories. As leaders we have a responsibility to protect the people who have been entrusted to our care and oversight. I am appalled at anyone who would abuse the gifts, but especially ministry leaders. Sadly, it happens more often than we would care to admit.

In my joint stewardship with my husband at Restoration Church, we have seen families who love the Lord and have strong biblical foundations return to church. Many have experienced hurt by way of leaders looking for control, while some hurt came as a result of people using prophecy to correct, admonish or shame. Through the healing process, hope and encouragement have been cultivated in places of hurt and offense. They have been restored and are rising up as strong pillars in our church.

I could hardly believe what I was hearing when a lady from our church shared her past experience with the prophetic. When she and her husband were new believers they attended a church that on occasion would dedicate an entire Sunday service to prophecy. It sounded intriguing until she said how they used the prophetic to call people out in front of everyone attending that morning. The prophetic leaders would tell certain individuals what was going on and what they were doing wrong. It was embarrassing for everyone. As this couple shared their experience with me they said, "We never got called out, but one time another woman did in regard to something she had done wrong against us. It caused us all embarrassment." The couple went on to share that the entire service they kept having these thoughts: *Oh please, don't let them choose me. Is God really like this? Why would God embarrass people this way?* This experience set a tone for their thinking regarding prophetic ministry and how God views His children. At that time, they had not been exposed to the healthy operation of the prophetic, nor did they understand the prophetic is to be used as a gift of encouragement, not reproach.

God gave us the gift of prophecy to reveal His nature. He never intended prophecy to draw a crowd. The prophetic culture today, however, is enticing. We are intrigued when someone moves in the prophetic, as though we are watching a high-wire stage act. Instead of drawing closer to God we hunger after the prophet. I am sorry to say I have been guilty of this very thing. I have chased after prophets and their words, and I knew better! My intention began innocently: to find confirmation and clarity of what God was telling them about me. If I could hear the words from a trusted prophet, I would believe—or so I thought.

God made it clear that what I had been taught about prophecy and my methods of teaching were creating a dependency on me instead of a dependency on Him. This idea challenged what I thought I knew about the prophetic. After God showed me the foundational importance of relationship I began to see how easy it was for people to become dependent on a prophet or a prophetic ministry. They were using it as a crutch.

Leading up to a prophetic conference at a well-known church, several people told me about their impressive ministry teams. At the time I was in a difficult place, and it would have been nice to get a word from the Lord to encourage me and confirm my direction. Not once during the entire three-day conference did they minister prophetically. I was a little irritated about this and asked God, "What's the deal?" His response was, *What do you think?*

Sheesh! I really do not like it when God answers my questions with a question. If I wanted to get a response from Him, I knew I was going to need to answer His question first. I prayed and shared my thoughts with God over the course of a few days, and He confirmed I was on the right track. Prophecy is not about the prophet. Period. It is about communication with God. I needed to get to a place in my relationship with Him where I trusted His words spoken directly to me.

To be fair, I do not think it is just me. I think many Christians do not believe God will speak directly to them. They may or may not believe God can speak to others—their friends, their families, a skier buried under an avalanche—but definitely not to them. They seek direction from others and fail to develop their own ears to hear from God.

Unfortunately, the prophetic culture can exploit our healthy and natural hunger for God. First, a word is given that leaves people hungry to hear more. Then they are given lip service to the idea that they too can hear God. It is like a crooked therapist who listens and proclaims, "See you next week!" with no intention of addressing the real areas of the patient's brokenness. Those of us who operate in the gift of prophecy are on very thin ice when we believe we should be the only ones delivering God's message rather than providing the tools for everyone to hear for themselves. The crippling result of seeking the prophet over God is the loss of personal relationship with Him and powerful freedom that this brings. Jesus invested Himself in His friends in order for them to have a relationship with the Father. That is what it is all about, isn't it?

When a prophetic culture is created that implies that though we can all hear God, some hear better than others, the tendency is to listen to the person who hears best. On the freeway of life, this is one exit ramp away from idol worship. Just as God did with Adam and Eve, He wants to speak to His people.

I realized I had become a stumbling block. I asked God to show me clearly what I needed to do. He said, *Get out of the way! Teach the people how to hear from Me, and step aside.* Since that lesson there is a balance. If the goal is to equip people with the tools to hear God and then kick them out of the nest to fly, then I am on board!

In a nutshell, it is a heart issue. If the intent is to foster a dependency on a person, then there is a big problem. God has called us to encourage one another. While we can give advice, help and lean on each other, God ultimately wants us leaning and depending upon Him and Him alone. God wants us to be obedient to speak what He reveals, all the while pointing people to Him.

In God's design, prophecy brings freedom. Is there anything more liberating than knowing who God is and what He wants to do in our lives? If we can learn to hear His voice, then we can confidently step out and obey His call on our lives. Why? Because that is what Jesus did. It is what He modeled for us, and it is what He has called us to do. John 8:47 (ESV) records that He said, "Whoever is of God hears the words of God." We can confidently expect to hear His voice when we listen for it.

I cannot say this any stronger: Do not chase after a prophetic word! Rather, chase after the Lord for answers. If God wants to speak to you via another person, I promise He will present you with opportunities and make sure the message gets through.

Go Deeper

- Have you seen misuse or abuse in the Church regarding prophecy? Explain.

- Have you ever sought a word instead of God?

- Have you ever had people come to you for things they should have been going to God for? How did you handle that situation? Looking back, should you have done anything differently?

Activation Prayer

God, help me to chase after You and You alone. Help me to be a good steward of the gifts and talents You have given me. Help me to look to You and not seek control or power for my own gain. Help me to trust in You, God, and the words that You speak to my heart. Help me to go deeper with You today and every day.

Activate Encouragement

Do you have a specific question or questions you want to hear from God about? If so, I want you to take time to write out each question. Then set aside time to write a "Dear Jesus" letter. Begin by writing, "Dear Jesus," and then write out your question as if you were asking it to Him directly. After that, listen to what the Holy Spirit is speaking to you and begin to write out what you hear. Do not pause to read it or stop to think about what you are writing. Just write. Once done, go back and read what you wrote and what the Spirit spoke to you. You can do this with each of your questions.

Encouragement in Action

The Dominican Republic

For several years I traveled twice a year to the Dominican Republic to minister and train people in hearing God's voice. On one particular trip I was able to spend more time teaching and encouraging people to hear God for themselves rather than simply ministering. In return, they received blessings from the Lord and from each other. It was seriously amazing!

The Lord also opened my eyes to a new revelation. He showed me the power of simply speaking over people so that He is revealed. This revelation led me to study 1 Corinthians 14:24–25:

> But if an unbeliever or an inquirer comes in while everyone is prophesying, they are convicted of sin and are brought under judgment by all, as the secrets of their hearts are laid bare. So they will fall down and worship God, exclaiming, "God is really among you!"

This Scripture truly came to life for me during this trip. I had the privilege of ministering to five young college students, all of whom I wrongly assumed were saved because they were in church. From my perspective, the prophetic words I shared with them during ministry did not seem to be anything extraordinary. Yet God revealed to each one that He knew them personally, and they were convinced they needed to have a personal relationship with Him.

Because of the language barrier I shared the words and pictures God gave me through an interpreter. One of the young ladies asked the interpreter, "How did she know those things about me?" Another said, "I want that thing she was talking about—that peace and transformation on the inside—because I don't have it, and I have been searching for it." They surrendered their lives to God not because I delivered any profound words but because God showed up and used me to speak to them personally.

We can all hear God. God is real; He speaks today, and His power touches lives. Brace yourself. I am going to say it again: We can hear God! We do not need big displays of ministry or thundering words of knowledge to have an impact in people's lives. We must simply dare to hear God and be obedient to share His message.

It has been said we may be the only Bible that most people read. If we tune our ear to the Father's heart we can touch the lives of people the Lord has been longing to call His own. This is why we should embody the attitude Paul described in Romans 1:16: "I am not ashamed of the gospel, because it is the *power* of God that brings salvation to everyone who believes" (emphasis added).

I have a friend, Karter, whom I call the coffee shop prophet/ evangelist. I believe God has enabled him to bring the message of salvation to the baristas in a 100-mile radius of where we live, in addition to those he meets in coffee shops on a regular basis. Last year he led 38 people to the Lord. In the first six months of this year alone he has led 40 to Christ. Every morning he heads to the coffee shop to have devotions before starting his day. During his breaks throughout the workday or on his travels he stops at coffee stands or shops. I guess you could say he likes coffee, but in truth he is there on assignment. He is definitely not afraid of the Gospel, or the power of God, but that was not always the case.

When I was first learning to operate in my prophetic gifting I was often paired with my friend Karter. He was prophetic then also but had a problem with fear—fear of rejection and the fear of man. He was afraid of what people would think if he shared with them a word of encouragement or even about Jesus. I vividly remember one time he wrote out a word for me, and it took him six months to give it to me. Had he given it to me when he had first received it, it would have ministered to me more deeply. I was still encouraged by it, but it spoke to some things I was going through six months prior.

Three years ago things changed for Karter as God began to show him that He wanted to use him in unconventional ways. Karter's job takes him out in the field, and he travels all over neighboring counties. God uses Karter to bring hope and life to people he meets every single day. Once Karter was sent to work in a location more than an hour away. While he was working, a 93-year-old war veteran who lived nearby came to see what he was doing. Karter immediately got a word of encouragement for him and asked the man if he could share it with him. As Karter gave him a word of encouragement, he could see pain in the man's eyes. This war veteran shared that he was on a ship in Pearl Harbor the day it was bombed and had lost many friends in the war that day. God gave Karter a word of knowledge and he said, "With all you've seen, I know you believe in God, but you've never asked Jesus into your heart, have you?" The man responded no, and Karter led him in the sinner's prayer.

Recently, Karter shared one of the most powerful testimonies I have heard to date. It is a testimony I believe embodies the purpose and reason we each need to embrace the gift of prophetic encouragement. On his day off Karter was waiting at a local coffee shop for his son to arrive when a young woman entered. The Lord immediately told him she needed an encouraging word. Karter started writing what the Lord was speaking to him, but he could see the young woman was about to leave. Karter whispered, "Lord, if You want her to receive this word, You'd better make sure she doesn't leave." Karter saw the young gal reach the door, pause, take a deep breath, turn around and take a seat at a table near the door. Karter walked to her table and handed her the piece of paper with the explanation that the Lord wanted to encourage her with these words. Karter always says, "If you read it and it's for you, then take it; if not, then toss it."

As he went back to his table he watched her reaction as she read the note. She began to wipe tears from her eyes, and then she began to sob. It broke Karter's heart, and he approached her, kneeling down by her table, and gently asked if she was okay. She responded, no, she was not. Her 22-year-old sister had unexpectedly died and left behind a 10-month-old child in her care. The child's father was never in the picture, and the grandparents were elderly. She felt all alone. As she shared her story with Karter she suddenly exclaimed, "I have no idea what I am doing or why I even sat down; I have to go to work!"

Karter shared with me the first line of the note: "You have faced tragedy, but God loves you and has a plan for you."

He said, "She was a 19-year-old girl who looked like she had it all together. I am so glad I listened to the prompting of the Lord that day, and I know all heaven is celebrating that she too said yes to Jesus."

Just as God opens doors for my friend Karter, He will open them for you and me. All we need to do is step through those doors and respond to what we hear the Lord speaking.

---------------------------------- **Activation Prayer** ----------------------------------

Jesus, I thank You that You are alive and moving today! Help me not to be ashamed of You or Your Gospel. May my life be a testimony and proof of Your power, truth and love to those whom I meet every day.

----------------------------------- **Go Deeper** -----------------------------------

- Revisit 1 Corinthians 14:24–25.

- Why do you think an unbeliever would show such a powerful response to a prophetic word?

- Ask yourself, *If my life were the only Bible others read, what would they see/hear/read?*

18

Heart Check

In a society that tells us it is all about us, it is easy to fall into
the trap of the enemy concerning issues of the heart. When
operating in any of the spiritual gifts we must be vigilant to
maintain a posture of humility and keep our eyes focused on
God. This is especially true regarding the gift of prophecy.

Prophecy is not about us. It is about what He wants revealed
to bring about obedience, encouragement and maturity in each
of us. All spiritual gifts are not about us; they are about the
heart of God for His people. When we operate in any gift of
the Spirit we are simply vessels to carry out God's plans and
purposes.

Even before I truly understood God had called me to the
prophetic I spent an entire year learning the importance of
humility the hard way. At the time I thought, *Wow, I must be
pretty slow*. Every Scripture I studied had to do with humility
and pride. Let's just say I was given many opportunities to get
it right. I finally figured out my specific assignment from the

Lord was to learn everything I could about how to minister while maintaining a posture of humility.

I do not think any of us sets out to be prideful. It is part of our sin nature and one of the ways the enemy assaults us. All of us have a need to be recognized and valued for who we are and what we bring to the table. Consequently, if we feed that need, allowing it to be the primary focus, then we lose ourselves down a slippery slope of pride.

If you read about the great men and women of our faith, you will see that many of them fell victim to issues of the heart. King David thought he could hide his sin from God. In the end God exposed his sin and his heart condition. In the following verse, King David shows us how to approach the Lord with a heart that is open to His leading.

> Search me, God, and know my heart; test me and know my anxious thoughts. See if there is any offensive way in me, and lead me in the way everlasting.
>
> Psalm 139:23–24

We cannot be effective vessels for God if our hearts are not right with Him. Be armed with the knowledge that your heart is the wellspring of life, and protect it. In Proverbs 4:23 King Solomon tells us, "Above all else, guard your heart, for everything you do flows from it."

The great commandment of the Bible is to "love the Lord your God with all your heart and with all your soul and with all your strength and with all your mind; love your neighbor as yourself" (Luke 10:27). When operating in the gifts, we must not be driven by our own personal agendas or motives. A pivotal theme of this book is the idea that the prophetic is misused and abused. In the majority of cases this abuse is unintentional. I am sure we would all like to think no one would speak a prophetic word that was not from God and say it was. But my experience contradicts this thought.

One situation that truly opened my eyes was when a trusted friend gave me a prophetic word. I was at a vulnerable time in ministry and on the verge of launching a conference, which had been a long-planted dream from God. The word initially seemed accurate, but there were elements that felt sharply judgmental and personal. I immediately had some red flags but discounted them because of my friendship with the person. I shared the word with my board members. One of them looked me straight in the eye and said, "Why don't you trust the discernment God gave you? You can clearly see this person has an ulterior motive to set you straight. This is not a word from the Lord but a word from this individual's flesh being passed as a word from the Lord." The red flags I sensed were not imagined; they were the result of the Lord impressing the truth upon my friend's heart and alerting me to the reality of that person's motive, just as the Word promises in Proverbs 21:2 (esv): "Every way of a man is right in his own eyes, but the Lord weighs the heart."

We must love others more than we love ourselves, and we must focus on God and direct others to Him. This is what God meant when He said to me, *The misuse and abuse of prophecy needs to stop.* If we corrupt what God intends to happen with our own agendas, over time it becomes impossible to discern the difference.

I am far from perfect. I often have to push past my own thinking to hear what God has to say. I currently serve as co-pastor with my husband at a community church. I have frequent opportunities to deliver prophetic words to church leaders and to churches corporately. When the Lord speaks a word about a particular situation, especially if it is one I am passionate about, I need to check my heart first. Sometimes it is difficult to separate myself from what the Lord is saying. At times I have very strong opinions, but I make every effort to prevent my personal opinions from impairing my hearing.

I have developed a simple checklist to follow before delivering a word.

1. Take ample time to pray, being careful not to rush the process.
2. Make sure personal thoughts or feelings do not taint the delivery of the message. When there is a chance it might mess up God's word, wait!
3. Examine my heart, attitude and motives in regard to the message by asking:
   a. How would this word strike me if I were receiving it?
   b. Are my words harsh or accusatory?
   c. Are my words tempered with love and truth?

I often partner with churches by providing prophetic teaching and counsel. One particular time while working with a church, the leadership desired to have the prophetic incorporated within its ministries. In doing so I mentored several members, but they did not know how to implement it effectively and responsibly within their church. That is where I came in.

One church member participated in one of my Dare 2 Hear classes and had been cautiously stepping out with positive results. One evening while praying for one of the church ministries, he began to receive a prophetic word of encouragement. As he wrote it down the encouraging tone shifted, and the word became harsh and opinionated.

The prophetic word that was written down and delivered was simply hurtful. It detailed an impending disaster within the church leadership, and it could not be stopped. Yikes! Was this God? Clearly I did not know the answer to this with total certainty, but I could pray and ask if it aligned with God's Word.

Was this person intentionally being hurtful? I believe it was a well-intended individual who got caught without a safety net. It is vital to take the time to pray and ask, *Is this me, or is this the Lord?* Most importantly, no one should ever deliver a negative word without a great deal of prayer and pastoral guidance.

When God does indeed speak a word of correction or warning He will usually give it to a trusted individual who has a relationship with the people involved. Why? So the word can be delivered from a heart of love and concern. If such a word is to be spoken and received, it has to come from a heart that is right—with no ulterior motive, agenda or malice.

Phoebe had an experience with someone who had a personal agenda and a strong opinion on what she thought Phoebe needed. In turn, this ministry leader used a supposed prophetic gifting to manipulate Phoebe to do what she thought best. Phoebe had volunteered to help run the soundboard once a week at a 12-step program for struggling Christians. Eventually she was asked to stay and attend the breakout session because "everyone struggles with something!" The pastor responsible for placing people into struggle-specific groups decided to place Phoebe into a low self-esteem group because she felt the Lord prompted her to do so. Phoebe, out of respect and trust, agreed. After a month, however, Phoebe decided it was not the right group for her. Thus began the series of group hopping. Each placement was because the pastor felt it was a good fit for Phoebe despite her never having experienced the struggles that others in the groups had.

During one ministry meeting Phoebe was asked how she was doing, and she finally admitted she felt like she was being bounced around. The ministry pastor was quick to end any further discussion in front of the whole staff. Months later Phoebe dropped the ministry altogether and started to walk through a real healing process. The one time Phoebe revisited the program was to be supportive for a friend sharing her testimony. As soon as she walked in the door the pastor exclaimed, "Oh, good! You're back! I'm so glad you're hearing from the

Lord." Phoebe left without saying a word as soon as her friend was done giving her testimony.

A healthy heart condition is essential to serve God. God has a plan and a purpose that will be accomplished. As we move in the gift of prophetic encouragement we have to keep our own ideas and biases from seeping into what the Lord is saying to us. This is the battlefield where a lot of people lie wounded. Very few people in ministry set out to corrupt. Once the door is opened, the enemy swoops in and perverts the gift God has given us. He will use jealousy. He will use the desire for recognition. He will use the love of money. He will use whatever he can to attack us. I have heard leaders say there are three paths to downfall: gold, glory and girls. In today's lingo we would probably call it the love of money, power and sex. It is an oversimplification perhaps, but it is absolutely true. After all, "Where your treasure is, there your heart will be also" (Luke 12:34).

Go Deeper

- When looking at the checklist in this chapter, is there something you would like to add before you give a word to someone else?

- Read Proverbs 21:2 and 1 Samuel 16:7. Why do you think God looks at the heart?

- Read Luke 12:22–34. In candidly assessing your life, do you have anxiety in any areas? Also, where would you say your treasure is? Do you think God would agree?

Activation Prayer

Pray aloud Psalm 139:23–24 from *The Message*: "*In-vestigate my life, O God, find out everything about me;*

cross-examine and test me, get a clear picture of what I'm about; see for yourself whether I've done anything wrong—then guide me on the road to eternal life."

Activate Encouragement

Take a prayer walk around your community and ask God to reveal what He wants you to see. Then record the information, including the date. Begin to speak words of prophecy over your community that line up with what God revealed. Continue these prayer walks, making sure to record any praise reports. You can do this same exercise and pray to receive words for your town, schools, government leaders, church leaders, etc.

Encouragement in Action

My most profound ministry times happen in the marketplace.* God uses these opportunities for us to introduce and connect Him to people. One of my favorite encounters was when my daughter and I went on a treasure hunt to Walmart. Now, I am not talking about *treasure* in terms of getting a great deal. I am talking about people. Nothing compares to the treasures God highlights in the form of people. Kevin Dedmon has a fantastic book titled *The Ultimate Treasure Hunt*, and if you have not read it then I highly recommend it. It is amazing! It forever changed my life. In it, Dedmon teaches that when you seek God and ask Him to reveal clues to lead you to your treasure, He will. Your treasure is someone who has a prayer need of some kind. Any need will do: healing, encouragement, confirmation—anything.

On this day my daughter, Brandi, and I took some time to hear from God, and then we came back together to share our impressions with each other. The following words were on my list: *beach towels*, *end cap* and *someone needing prayer for foot or leg pain*. My daughter showed me her list and said, "Mom, I don't think I am hearing very well today." She had four words: *bananas*, *windows*, *headaches* and *martini glasses*. I was amused and asked her if she even knew what a martini glass was. She shook her head no. I also wondered if she was hearing God.

When we arrived at Walmart our attention was drawn to two ladies in the parking lot with several kids. We headed inside, and I asked my daughter where she wanted to start first. She said we should go to the bananas because they were at the front of the store.

As we walked in that direction we noticed the same lady who caught our attention while we were outside. We decided not to approach her because she was talking on her phone. My daughter was not convinced she was the treasure. We went in search of

---

The marketplace refers to any place other than in the church building. It is anywhere I may go about my normal, day-to-day activities or a location in the community God may specifically direct me.

the beach towels. As we located the shelf with the beach towels we found an end cap in the same row with martini glasses. My daughter got excited and repeated, "What do we do? What do we do? I can't believe this!" I calmly told her we were going to have to wait until someone passed our way. Our clues were right on, and our treasure would come to us.

As we drifted up and down the beach towel aisle trying not to look peculiar, an older gentleman and his wife passed by. He was limping, so I thought perhaps he was my treasure. We followed them to the section with foot products. It is actually rather difficult not to look like a stalker when, in fact, you are stalking. I greeted him, introduced myself and Brandi, and then said, "We are on a treasure hunt. I don't want or need anything from you other than a few minutes of your time to talk." I showed him my treasure map of clues and then explained why I believed he was the specific treasure to which God had directed me. I asked if he would allow us to pray for him, and he agreed.

Then it was my daughter's turn. I was trying to figure out the clue about windows. Walmart does not have windows in their stores, so I began to question her: "When you got 'bananas,' what came to mind? The actual bananas or something else?" Her response surprised me. "Well, I kept thinking banana split, but that makes no sense unless it's banana split ice cream." That was it! I realized the windows she had written down on her treasure map were actually the doors in the cold food section.

We headed toward the ice cream in search of banana split. We were standing in front of the ice cream when the same two ladies with the kids came walking toward us. I asked my daughter what she thought. She said, "Yep, I think she's the one. She's our headache lady."

We approached them in the same way we had the man we met in the aisle with the foot products. "Hi, I am Debbie, and I'm on a treasure hunt," I explained. "I don't want anything from you, but I believe you are the treasure I am looking for. Again, I don't want anything from you other than to talk for a few minutes." I showed her our clues and asked her if she suffered with headaches. She responded, "Yes, I have a brain tumor, and unfortunately it gives me constant headaches." Wow! I asked if she would let us pray for her, and she hesitantly agreed. We prayed for her right there next to the banana split ice cream in the middle of the frozen foods section at Walmart. God is amazing!

The story doesn't end there. After we finished she looked me straight in the eye and said, "Are you Foursquare?" I was startled a little by her tone, but I simply replied, "Yes, in fact, I am a Foursquare pastor." She held her stare and said, "I don't really do the whole church thing, and I don't believe what you believe."

I told her that was totally okay; God sent us to her, and He loved her. He wanted her to be prayed for and healed. She replied, "I asked if you were Foursquare because my sister-in-law is, and your prayer reminded me of her prayer when my doctor told me I couldn't have children." She nodded her head toward a bench at the end of the aisle and said, "That little girl is my daughter. I conceived her after being prayed over." I just stood there for a minute. "Well, God wanted you to know He cares for you enough to send us and remind you of what He has done in the past. When the brain tumor is gone you will know it was God who healed you."

Lady from Walmart, if you are reading this, I would love to hear from you.

Linda shared her story about her treasure hunt and how she questioned whether or not she was hearing God. Her clues were *flip-flops*, *health food section* and *prayer for a fear they had*. Linda and her partner walked through most of Walmart and saw no one wearing flip-flops. There was not a particular health food section at this store, but they decided the pharmacy had vitamins. As they rounded the corner to the pharmacy, bingo, there was a young woman wearing flip-flops. She had a baby in her cart. They walked up to her and told her they were on a treasure hunt and she was the treasure! They asked if they could pray for her about anything she feared. She said she was afraid the father of her baby would try to get custody of her little girl, and he was an abusive person. Linda asked her if they could pray for her, and she agreed. The young woman was very touched, and so was Linda. In fact, Linda has her name and the baby's written down in her prayer book and will pray for them as the Lord brings them to mind.

There is more to the testimony Mark Gilbaugh, the former Army medivac pilot, shared in chapter 7 that bears mentioning here. On the very last night of my classes I always do a fun activation for the adults and kids. For the adults, I send them out into the community on treasure hunts looking for people needing prayer. For the children, I have them hunt for literal treasure chests in the building.

Enjoy reading Mark's experience in his own words:

For our last Dare 2 Hear class activation we did a treasure hunt.

In the classroom I prayed for clues to find my treasure. God revealed to me that my treasure was a person struggling with pain in their feet. I asked God to show me how to find my treasure. He showed me a picture of a yellow sundress. I thought this final assignment was going to become mission: impossible since we were in the middle of a November rainstorm.

We drove down the road to the local Walmart in search of our treasures. The rest of my teammates found their treasures quickly, and we prayed for these people as we encountered them. With time running out, my confidence in finding my treasure waned. I felt I misheard God and prepared to go home empty-handed, but my team would not let me give up.

We walked outside, and as we passed Supercuts I saw a lady wearing a yellow dress cutting hair. I could not believe it. I knew this person was the treasure God had pointed out in my prophetic picture, but I was standing outside the window staring like a creeper. My teammates urged me, "Get in there!"

Two ladies from our team went in with me to help with the awkwardness. I greeted the woman in the yellow dress and explained, "We believe God speaks today, and He sent me here to give you an encouraging word." I asked if she was having pain in her feet. She responded, "Yes, I go home every night with aching feet because I stand all day."

At last, I had found my treasure! God really did speak to me!

With her permission we prayed over her and her feet. We prayed that God would reveal Himself to her in a real way and that she would know God loved her enough to send crazy people specifically to her.

I do not know what happened to this woman, but I do not have to know. Whatever the reason, God needed this one woman in the millions of people living in the area to know that He saw her. He saw her right where she was. He knew her pain, and He loved her enough to send some encouragement.

When we take the time to hear from God, not only does He use this time to encourage us, but He wants us to encourage the hurting people around us. God does not expect me to understand what is going on in their lives; He simply asks for our obedience.

While Mark and his wife were out in the community searching for their treasures in the form of people, their children were at the church hunting for their treasure boxes. Each child was to seek the Lord for a word or a picture of where their specific box was hidden. I did not hide them, so I could help the kids discern what they were hearing without my own knowledge getting in the way.

Andrew, Mark's son, had a similar experience at the same time. Here is his story:

> I was upstairs in the kids' class, and we had just recited the Old Testament books in order when they turned the lights off and told us to pray. I was very doubtful that it would work, but I did what every other kid was doing. Then I started thinking about guitar, and my mind dozed off. As the kids started to walk downstairs I realized maybe I should actually start praying and focus. Then I saw a rain forest with a fallen tree. I thought I was seeing things, and I kept praying for a few minutes hoping I would get a "real" word/picture. I could not stop thinking about the fallen tree.
>
> I headed downstairs, and as soon as I turned the corner I saw a tree. I immediately walked over to it. I can still remember the feeling that it was actually my treasure and had my name on it. It was a wooden treasure box filled with chocolate candy wrapped in a coin wrapper and a plastic beaded necklace. There was also a written prophetic word just for me. My faith in Jesus would not be the same without that class. Every time I lose something I pray that God will give me a picture of where it is. That class (when I was six) changed the way I saw everything from then on.

Another child had drawn a picture of a large circle that he colored in completely dark. It was the only clue he had. He searched and searched, and while others were finding their treasures, he was not. I encouraged him to go back and seek God again, asking for more. While I was helping another child I heard commotion coming from the sanctuary and came in to find this five-year-old boy loudly cheering. He had found his treasure in the large, round kick drum! What a story he was able to share with others about how God showed him specifically where his treasure was. Even though at first he did not understand where God was leading, God was faithful to answer when he came back for more clarity.

The same is true for us. If at first we do not understand, it is okay to ask for more clarity. I recently had someone ask, "Why doesn't God speak specifically and clearly?" I told her in truth I was not one hundred percent sure, but in my heart I feel as if God wants us to search for the hidden treasures in the Kingdom. As we search for His truth He will reveal (see Matthew 13:34–35) and make known to us the deeper spiritual messages often overlooked by those not following after Him.

--------------------- **Activation Prayer** ---------------------

Father, give me Your eyes to see the treasures in people, and help me to see them the way You do. Help me be sensitive to times when Your Spirit is moving and asking me to be an encouragement to those I do not know.

----------------------- **Go Deeper** -----------------------

- Read Romans 1:16.

- Are you ashamed/afraid to share the truth of the Gospel with others? Why or why not?

- How do you think God will use you to encourage His "treasures"?

19

Embracing the Lifestyle of Encouragement

Remember, God wants to communicate with us as He did with Jesus when He walked on earth. Jesus' relationship with the Father is prophecy in action. This is a legacy Jesus left for you and me, and it is a legacy I want to leave for my children and future generations to come. It begins with you and me today! We have been given the mission to mentor and pass on the spiritual inheritance and knowledge that God bestowed upon us.

An inheritance in the natural helps us to start out ahead. It gives us a better position for moving forward. Don't we want that for our children? For the people we lead? For the people of God? I have been blessed with spiritual mothers and fathers, mentors who have faithfully and patiently invested their time and wisdom in me, cultivating the gifts God placed in my heart. Jesus did this very thing for His disciples. In today's society, formal mentoring is almost nonexistent. It is a lost art. The ceiling we look up to should be the next generation's floor. It is the biblical picture of inheritance Jesus imparted to us. We pay the price for the inheritance that future generations will get for free. In turn, they will do the same for the generations who follow after them. Every move of God, everything in the natural that we have, is because someone paid a price for it, starting with Jesus.

I am very grateful for the mentors who poured into me while allowing me to mature in the gifts God placed within me. With their encouragement I have grown in confidence of who I am in Christ, my true identity. Their encouragement put the courage in me to pursue all God has for me. We need to encourage others to grow into who God has called them to be. We do this by using the gift of prophetic encouragement to inspire and call forth the treasure hidden within.

The natural tendency is to look back over our history, our experiences and the things we have been taught for guidance. The unrealized mistake is that if we do not look for God in our tomorrows or in new ways we may miss Him. The Bible is full of stories of men and women who struggled with some of the same issues we do today. They often missed God until after the fact or because they were relying on past experiences.

Scriptures depict God showing up in all sorts of ways to speak out His plans for us. In the Old Testament He spoke to Moses through a burning bush and to the prophet Elijah through His quiet whisper. Today is no different. He can speak through all those methods, but He is not limited to them. We need to make sure our preconceived ideas or expectations do not become an obstacle to hearing God and developing a deeper relationship with Him. He wants to talk to you, and if you only expect Him to call out from a fiery bush it is certainly possible you will miss Him when He stops by to visit.

> Forget about what's happened; don't keep going over old history. Be alert, be present. I'm about to do something brand-new. It's bursting out! Don't you see it? There it is! I'm making a road through the desert, rivers in the badlands.
>
> Isaiah 43:18–19 MESSAGE

You may be asking, Where do I go from here? How do I use the gift of prophetic encouragement in my life? How do I recognize when He is speaking? The answer is to learn how God communicates with you and to activate the gift of prophetic encouragement in your life. Go on a journey with God to a deeper relationship. Take time to repeat the Activate Encouragement sections often. I promise it will forever change your life and the lives of those you meet.

Finally, I encourage you to document the words God speaks to you and keep them in a place where you can see them often. It is important to remind yourself of the plans and promises God has spoken to you to combat discouragement. Just as David encouraged himself in the Lord, you can too.

Now is the time to rise up and embrace the lifestyle of prophetic encouragement. It is time to change the course of your life and the people around you!

Go Deeper

- Read Matthew 28:18–20 and Mark 16:15–18. What revelation or truths can you glean today from these Scriptures with regard to what God has called all His followers to do?

- Read 1 Thessalonians 5:11. How can you apply this verse to your life every day?

Activation Prayer

Holy Spirit, come! Open my eyes, ears and heart to the new things You want to do in and through me. I am Your willing vessel. I want to exercise the gift of prophetic encouragement with those I meet every day!

Activate Encouragement

Begin by praying and asking God to dispatch you to someone in need of prayer. Ask God where you are to go, who you are looking for and what they need prayer for. Write these things down. Before you go, pray for God to orchestrate a divine encounter and give you words to speak. Now go on a treasure hunt!

Appendix 1

Quick Reference Guide

What is prophecy anyway?

Paul tells us he wants us all to desire spiritual gifts eagerly but to especially desire the gift of prophecy (see 1 Corinthians 14:1–5). Prophecy strengthens, encourages and comforts those who hear and receive it. The great news is this gift is for all.

The word *prophecy* can either mean "calling forth and declaring God's plans" or it can speak of future events. Often when people are operating with the spiritual gift of prophecy it is used in harmony with a word of wisdom or a word of knowledge.

Definitions

Prophesy

To foretell or forth-tell events beforehand; to speak forth a declaration inspired by and revealed by the Lord; to foretell or predict the future

Foretell

"To tell of beforehand, predict, prophesy";* to speak out revelation of what God will cause to happen

Forth-tell

To declare revelations, to call forth; to call into existence

Spiritual Gift of Prophecy

Speaking a Holy Spirit–inspired, timely word of edification, exhortation or comfort to individuals (see 1 Corinthians 14:3)

Word of Knowledge

God revealing something about a person or situation only God could know; can be about a situation that took place in the past or is currently taking place

Word of Wisdom

The Holy Spirit revealing God's will and God's solution in a situation or circumstance; knowledge rightly applied

What is the gift of prophetic encouragement?

Prophetic encouragement is the spiritual gift of prophecy in action, which Paul talks about in 1 Corinthians 14. Prophetic encouragement is intended for those who believe in Jesus, who listen to what heaven wants to say and encourage other believers and unbelievers alike (see 1 Corinthians 14:3–5, 24). Prophetic encouragement releases the heart of the Father into people's lives and situations. Take up the calling in 1 Thessalonians 5:11,

*Definition quoted from Dictionary.com.

which says, "Therefore encourage one another and build each other up, just as in fact you are doing."

What is "a word," and what does it mean to give a word?

When I refer to a "word" or "delivering a word" I am referring to a downloaded message from God to a person with the intent of sharing it with others. In prophetic circles, a word can mean any message from God represented as an impression, picture, vision, Scripture or a literal word.

There are two words in the Greek language used to translate the term *word* in the Bible. These Greek words are *logos* and *rhema*.

Logos Words

The Bible, from Genesis to Revelation, is filled with Scripture after Scripture called *logos* words. *Logos* is a Greek word that simply means "a universal word, a word that is for everyone." *Logos* refers to an expression (articulation) of thought.

The exciting thing about God is how He takes a message that is for everyone, like the Bible (*logos* word), and then personalizes the message for each individual, making it a *rhema* word.

Rhema Words

A *rhema* word is a personal word. It is a word taken from Scripture and applied to your personal circumstance. *Rhema* words are specific promises to a specific person at a specific time to accomplish a specific thing. When you receive a *rhema* word, you need to write it down, date it and place it where you will see it. Do not take your eyes off it. Your *rhema* word will help you see what is ahead and help you navigate those unexpected bumps and turns in the road.

Is there a formula to hear from God?

No. We are all different, and God speaks to each one of us in a unique way. There is no one-recipe-fits-all to hear from God.

As we strengthen the bond of our relationship with Him, we in turn will be tuned in to His voice. Remember Jesus' promise in John 10:5, 27: "My sheep will hear and know My voice, and the voice of another they will not follow."

It is out of the overflow of our relationship with Him that we develop a deep and genuine love to hear God's heart and share it with others.

What's the difference between Old Testament and New Testament prophecy?

A lot! In the beginning Adam and Eve had authentic relationship and communication with God. Then sin entered, and God chose prophets to hear from Him and relay His message. In short, the Old Testament was under the covenant of the Law. The New Testament, however, is the covenant of grace. In the New Testament we read how God restored to every person the ability to hear from Him. When God sent the Holy Spirit He restored prophecy to its original intent.

If I prophesy, does that make me a prophet?

No, it does not.

What is a prophet?

Biblically, a prophet is a person with a calling from God, and this person fulfills the office of prophet, which is a job description. (All of the fivefold offices outlined in Scripture in

198

Ephesians 4:11–13 are job descriptions from God to equip the saints.) If you are called to the office of prophet, then you have a responsibility to equip God's people for the work of ministry.

Who should be operating in prophecy?

Everyone! We are all prophetic. We can all prophesy. In the New Testament Paul tells us:

> For you can all prophesy in turn so that everyone may be instructed and encouraged. The spirits of prophets are subject to the control of prophets. For God is not a God of disorder but of peace—as in all the congregations of the Lord's people.
>
> 1 Corinthians 14:31–33

What do you do when you get a prophetic word for leadership?

For a complete answer to this question, read the Think on It! section titled "Getting Words for Others, Including Leaders" after chapter 13, as well as chapter 18, "Heart Check."

Why is there so much confusion surrounding prophecy today?

As discussed throughout this book, there are many reasons for confusion around prophecy. Satan sets traps to ensnare us and keep us from operating in prophecy. There is power in the gift of prophecy to set people free!

What does it mean to test/judge prophetic words?

Judging prophecy simply means testing everything of a spiritual nature and holding it up against the Word of God to discern if it is truth. For additional details, read chapter 9, "Put It on the Altar: Testing Prophecy."

What is a false prophet?

A person who speaks incorrectly or speaks untrue things is not necessarily a false prophet. What makes a person a false prophet is the underlying motive to deceive. As recorded in Acts 16:16–18, a slave girl followed Paul around. What she spoke was the truth; nonetheless, she clearly was not operating under the Spirit of God but a false spirit. Her motives were not pure.

Because we now live under the new covenant of grace, if we stoned those who got it wrong we would all be dead. We no longer live under the Law but under grace. God spoke through His prophets in the Old Testament because His people did not want direct interaction with Him. In the New Testament and today we have been given the Holy Spirit, and He speaks to all of us.

What do I do when I get it wrong?

There are many factors and reasons why we may get it wrong. One main reason is lack of experience and understanding in the ways God speaks. The main thing is to remain in humility and operate from a heart of love and encouragement. Please read chapter 12, "Help Wanted: ~~Perfect~~ Ordinary People Only," and chapter 13, "Missing the Mark," for more on what to do when you get it wrong.

What does it mean to practice the prophetic?

I often teach workshops on hearing the voice of God in our lives and how to operate in the spiritual gift of prophecy. During these workshops I have hands-on activations, or practice times, with a variety of exercises designed to acclimate people to the voice of the Lord. This takes place in a safe environment, with a small group of three to five people ministering to one another. I use the word *practice* because, like gaining competency in anything, people who are not used to hearing from God need some time to discern what information is from Him and what is not. In this safe place of stepping out to hear God and speak to others we learn to extend a lot of grace and love.

Appendix 2

Entering into Relationship with God

Building a relationship with Jesus Christ is not always easy. This is not because Jesus asks us to do the hard work but because we struggle with submitting our will to God's. It is hard work to build a foundation on a rock, but it is well worth the effort in the end.

> You are like a smart carpenter who built his house on solid rock. Rain poured down, the river flooded, a tornado hit—but nothing moved that house. It was fixed to the rock.
>
> Matthew 7:24–25 MESSAGE

Fixing yourself to Jesus Christ, the Rock, is worth the time and effort. Take a moment and consider which foundation you are built upon. Are you built on the sand in a house made of cards? "When a storm rolled in and the waves came up, it collapsed like a house of cards" (Matthew 7:27 MESSAGE). Or are you built on the solid Rock? When the "rain poured down, the river flooded . . . but nothing moved that house."

In order to exchange your sandy foundation for a strong, sturdy one that is built upon the Rock, you must believe. Believe that God sent His Son, Jesus, to die for you, that He rose on the third day and that He is in heaven preparing a place for you. He sent the Holy Spirit to be our Helper, our Guide, and to lead us into all truth until He returns again for those who have chosen to have a relationship with Him. Ask Jesus Christ into your heart today. Also pray to receive the baptism of the Holy Spirit.* He longs to have a real relationship with you, and your life will be forever changed!

Prayer of Salvation

Father God, I acknowledge I am a sinner in need of a Savior. Thank You for sending Your Son, Jesus, to die on the cross in my place and for my sins. Forgive me of my sins and for living my life selfishly. Jesus, thank You for Your loving sacrifice and giving of Yourself. Jesus, I ask that You come and live in me today. Thank You for sitting at the right hand of the Father, interceding just for me. I am grateful that You are preparing a place for me to be with You there. Thank You for sending Your Holy Spirit to be with me here on earth so I do not have to do life alone or in my own strength. Create in me a hunger for Your words and Your truth. Fill me with Your Spirit. I love You, Lord, and thank You for loving me too.

In Jesus' name I pray, Amen!

---

*A prayer to receive the Holy Spirit may be found in appendix 3.

Appendix 3

Baptism of the Holy Spirit

If you have never heard about or prayed to receive the Holy Spirit baptism, here are basic steps to follow. Perhaps the most important thing to know is it is a free gift, a gift that will change your life and clothe you with power to step out boldly to do the things God has called you to do. Before going further, I suggest you read Acts 2 in its entirety to see what happens when we are clothed with the Holy Spirit.

How to Pray for and Receive the Baptism of the Holy Spirit

1. Pray and remove any hindrances, such as:
   a. Sin
   b. Unforgiveness (see Matthew 18:21–35; Ephesians 4:32)
   c. Wrong teaching (see Hosea 4:6)
   d. Open spiritual doors giving the enemy access (see 1 Peter 5:8; Matthew 13)
2. Understand it is a free gift. You cannot earn it.

3. Believe by faith you will receive the gift the moment you ask.

4. Pray and ask God to give you the free gift of the Holy Spirit and the ability to speak in tongues, a heavenly language you have not learned. Also ask Him to clothe you in His power and strength. (See the "Prayer to Receive the Holy Spirit" below.)

5. Begin speaking words of praise and adoration to God and thank Him for the free gift you are about to receive.

6. Relax and allow the Holy Spirit to fill your mouth with words and sounds (not English). It may even sound like gibberish, similar to a baby when he's learning to talk. (This is completely normal. It is part of the process when you are willing to have faith like a child.)

7. Once you begin speaking in a new language, continue on for at least several moments.

8. Remember, tongues is one of the great gifts that comes with the Holy Spirit baptism. It is *an* evidence, not *the* evidence.

9. Continue to pray, develop and exercise this new language as often as possible.

Prayer to Receive the Holy Spirit:

God, I believe You have given the Holy Spirit to help me live life here on earth to the fullest for Your Kingdom! I receive the free gift of Your Holy Spirit and ask right now for the Holy Spirit to come upon me. Holy Spirit, fill me and clothe me with Your power and strength. I also ask that You give me the ability to speak in tongues, a heavenly spiritual language. I ask that You protect my mind and heart as I step out daily, fully equipped with Your Spirit to fulfill what You would have me to do.